Charles Dicken's

Hard Times Companion

Includes Study Guide, Historical Context, and Character Index

BOOKCAPS

A BookCaps™ Study Guide

www.bookcaps.com

Cover Image © Nongnuch Leelaphasuk - Fotolia.com

Table of Contents

About

We all need refreshers every now and then. Whether you are a student trying to cram for that big final, or someone just trying to understand a book more, BookCaps can help. We are a small, but growing company, and are adding titles every month.

Visit www.bookcaps.com to see more of our books, or contact us with any questions.

Historical Context

Childhood and youth—Charles Dickens was born in 1812 in Portsmouth, in the southern central coastal area of England, to John and Elizabeth Dickens. By the time he was ten, his family had already moved twice and now resided in Camden, in North London. When Charles was twelve, his father landed in debtor's prison for three months, owing to his inability to support his large family on his small income as a Naval clerk. He was followed soon afterwards by his wife and Charles's three youngest siblings. Charles had to temporarily leave school to work in a boot-blacking factory. When his father was released after receiving an inheritance from his mother's death, Charles returned to school, this time to the Wellington House Academy.

Early career—At fifteen, he worked as an administrative assistant for a lawyer. By 1829, he had learned shorthand and begun working as a reporter, eventually establishing himself as a Parliamentary reporter (essentially a transcriptionist) in 1831 for the *Mirror of Parliament,* a weekly documentation of Parliamentary debates. In 1834, he began working for the *Morning Chronicle* as a journalist.

Love and Marriage—At seventeen, Dickens fell in love with Maria Beadnell, a banker's daughter. The relationship lasted four years, until 1833, in part failing because of her family's objections. Three years later, he married Catherine Hogarth, whose father, George Hogarth, edited the *Evening Chronicle,* and with whom Dickens would father ten children. In 1857, he fell in love with the young actress, Ellen Ternan, which caused a final separation between his wife and himself a year later. Dickens and Ternan's relationship was not public, and they burned all related letters, but in his will, Dickens left Ternan enough money to support her for the remainder of her life.

Writing career—In 1833, at twenty-one years of age, Dickens first story, "A Dinner at Poplar Walk" appeared in the *Monthly Magazine.* This would be the beginning of his rapid success as a writer. From there he went on to publish *Sketches by Boz* (his pen name) and *The Pickwick Papers,* which originally came out in serial form, a technique he was to use for many of his ensuing works. This was the beginning of his prolific output as an author as well as an editor and, in some cases, publisher of various journals, including *Bentley's Miscellany* (1836-1839), *Master Humphrey's Clock* (1840-1841),

Household Words (1850-1859), and *All the Year Round* (1859-1870). Major works, often initially published in serial form, included *Oliver Twist* (1838), *Nicholas Nickleby* (1839), *The Olde Curiosity Shoppe* (1840), *Barnaby Ridge* (1841), and *A Christmas Carol* (1843). Dickens so-called dark period, considered to be his mature period, began in 1848 with the publication of *Donbey and Son,* followed by twenty years of an extraordinary creative output that would include such masterpieces as *David Copperfield, A Tale of Two Cities,* and *Great Expectations.* The novel *Hard Times* (1854) was written during this period. His last work, *The Mystery of Edwin Drood,* was interrupted by his death in 1870.

Conditions of the times—Most of Dickens's career took place during Queen Victoria's reign, which began in 1837, when Dickens was in his mid-twenties. Contemporary circumstances in England included severe working conditions, child labor, underemployment, and industrialization, which produced significant changes in the economy and labor conditions. Dickens's work as a newspaper, court, and Parliamentary reporter would have thoroughly familiarized him with contemporary events and, coupled with his detailed knowledge of London, provided food for his stories.

Political and charitable involvement—Dickens himself was passionately opposed to the horrible working conditions of the times, and in 1841, he openly protested the laws that sustained them. In 1847, having returned to London after spending time abroad, he responded to a request for help from Lady Angela Burdett-Coutts, a philanthropist and one of England's wealthiest heiresses. Her idea was to help establish Urania Cottage, a home where former prostitutes could learn a new way of life. Dickens managed the home for a decade. Around 1850, he became involved in amateur theater, which included many performances for charity.

Miscellaneous—In 1842, Dickens and his wife went on a first tour to America, but even though the author was well received, his impressions of the country were negative, and that in turn had a negative effect on his popularity. In 1844, the Dickens family spent a year in Genoa, Italy, followed about a year later by six months in Switzerland and Paris, after which they returned to London. In 1858, Dickens began giving public readings, which benefited him economically but wore him down physically, costing him his health. In 1865, on his way back to London from Paris, Dickens, Ternan, and Ternan's mother were involved in the Staplehurst rail accident, a serious train disaster that resulted in the derailment of most cars, though it spared their own. The experience had a deep effect on Dickens. In 1867, he embarked on a second hectic tour of the United States, which had to be limited to the East coast because of his failing health. He was again well received, in spite of his earlier negative statements on American ways. Back in London in 1868, he embarked on a final tour of farewell public readings, which also had to be interrupted for health reasons. He died of a stroke on June 9, 1870, the same date as the Staplehurst rail disaster five years earlier. He is buried in Westminster Abbey's Poet's Corner.

Plot Summary

On the surface, *Hard Times* is a story about certain key members of the Gradgrind family and those who become closely connected with them as their lives develop. The story is set in Coketown, a fictional industrial town in England, during the Industrial Age. The railroad was still relatively new, working conditions for the average person were deplorable, and pollution—both in terms of noise and grime—was extreme. So was the division between rich and poor, and the poor were viewed with little compassion or understanding.

Mr. Gradgrind, one of the wealthier residents of Coketown, has been closely watching and training his own and the rest of Coketown's children to think of nothing but useful facts, facts, facts. Any sense of wonder, imagination, or emotion was to be speedily dealt with and discarded. Things like love, enjoyment, and generosity were simply not considered other than to point out their uselessness. Entertainment and imagination were similarly not allowed to be a part of life. Even normally simple descriptions of things such as horses had to have a factual, scientific bent, or they were considered unlearned and off the mark.

As the story unfolds, the results of this type of thinking become apparent. Those trained in the factual way of thinking have difficulty connecting with their own emotions, leading them to make poor life decisions that eventually result in unhappiness and, in some cases, disaster. Louisa, Mr. Gradgrind's eldest daughter and favorite child, reluctantly marries Josiah Bounderby, an egotistical "self-made" man who is one of Coketown's wealthiest and most successful citizens. He, too, is a believer in the "facts" philosophy and is a close friend of Mr. Gradgrind. He takes on Gradgrind's eldest son, Tom, as an apprentice; but Tom's utter lack of moral structure (morals were not facts) eventually turns him into a thief, liar, and fugitive. Louisa's stability, too, is almost totally toppled by the advances of one of her father's and husband's business associates, Mr. James Harthouse, who falls in love with her and tries to convince her to break her marriage vows. She finds herself on shaky moral and emotional ground, and in desperation she flees to her father's home, where she pleads for him to save her—but with what? His philosophy led her to this place … how can it possibly save her? Seeing his favorite child, the pride of his system, in this distressed condition, he begins to rethink his approach. Through his experience of this and a number of other events, he ultimately concludes that facts by themselves are not enough and that there is an indefinable quality, called love, that must inform life with a greater sense of humanity and charity.

The story is fleshed out by a number of subplots, including that of the abandoned circus rider's daughter, Sissy Jupe, who is taken in and raised by the Gradgrind family; the colorful expressiveness of the horse riders' ring leader, Mr. Sleary, and his group of entertainers; the stories of certain "Hands"—Coketown's hardworking mill workers (in this case, at a weaving mill)—whose simplicity and benevolence contrast markedly with the coldness and amorality of most of the fact-driven group; the jaded, amoral attitudes of the refined out-of-towner, Mr. James Harthouse; the petty concerns and vindictiveness of Mr. Bounderby's highborn housekeeper, Mrs. Sparsit; and the mysterious old woman, who appears periodically near Bounderby's mansion and whose identity is only revealed later in the novel.

All these subplots play into the central concept that human beings need greater motives for their existence than pure self-interest and worldly success—that without a deeper sense of love and truth, and without the human ingredients of wonder and imagination, a life can easily lack meaning, joy, and purpose. It is an openly Christian interpretation as is clear from the titles of the different Books and from certain sections of the novel where the origin of Dickens's philosophy becomes unmistakable. He regularly makes references to the Bible, but his references never overwhelm the story, and they are integrated in a way that, especially in the context of Victorian England, would seem natural and normal. Today, in a more multicultural time, they might stand out from the text. Alternatively, for those who are ignorant of the specifics of Christian thinking, their source might not be so obvious. It is a tribute, however, to the Christian religion as it was understood by Dickens, that the thoughts and values based on its teachings have such timeless, universal resonance that even the most religiously ignorant reader will draw much that is worthwhile from the book and will hopefully come away from it a richer, more humane person.

Key Concepts

The one thing needful

The source of this phrase is the story in the New Testament where Martha complains to Jesus that Mary is neglecting her duties while Martha does all the work serving the guests. Jesus' loving reply to Martha is to release her worries about material needs, for Mary, he tells her, has chosen the "one thing … needful"—the spiritual. As the title of Dickens's first chapter, this is obviously meant to be tongue in cheek. The orientation of Coketown's leading citizens is anything but spiritual as they do their best to choke the seeds of imagination and wonder with facts, facts, facts.

The inadequacy of worldly wisdom

Despite the success it brings to those willing to sell their souls to its concepts, the worldly wisdom of Coketown's fact men creates a gaping void in the lives of those who, for one reason of another, buy into its philosophy. It allows for no imagination, no wonder, no self-expression or amusement, and little in the way of enjoyment. Its mode is calculation; it's focus, so-called hard facts; it's motivation, self-interest. It is a clear recipe for unhappiness.

The power of love

This is perhaps the most prominent theme of the book. It stands in stark juxtaposition to the cold materialism of the fact-minded men who govern Coketown. It is not the recipe for worldly success, but it has an undeniable power of its own—a power that can supersede the amorality and self-interest that often accompany the worldly mindset. Its power rests in its essential residence in the human soul as a key ingredient for happiness. What the fact-men missed was that love is a human need that will eventually assert itself, just as the flames burst forth in the night from Coketown's chimneys.

As you sow, so shall you reap

This is another fundamental principle of Christianity that is immediately evident in the titles of the first two of the novel's three main books: *Sowing* and *Reaping.* The point is that it is not only our actions that produce inevitable results but our thinking. The thoughts we adopt inform our lives by shaping how we approach our own minds and emotions, which in turn affects our relationships and decisions. Here, Dickens does not sugarcoat things but creates a story in which each character's ultimate fate is the logical outcome, both materially and spiritually, of the character's choices and history.

Sifting the wheat from the chaff

This principle is also called "garnering," and it is the title and main subject of the third of *Hard Times'* books. It is a continuation of the sowing and reaping analogy, and it refers to the New Testament parable of the wheat and the tares, in which both the bad and good crops have grown up side by side and are now being separated, the one to be stored, the other to be destroyed. Dickens's take on this is not to be purely understood in terms of the characters' lives, but of how their thoughts and beliefs ultimately affected their lives: in the end, the good in their thinking survived, while the selfish and untrue was destroyed.

The humble shall be exalted, and the proud shall be brought low

Similar to the previous concept, the main idea here is that those who (especially falsely) exalt themselves will fall by the weight of their own actions, while those who follow a humble, truthful path will gain accordingly, either in happiness, stability, or some other benefit. Again, Dickens does not try to oversimplify what that means in practice. Those who choose good do not necessarily achieve great wealth and live happily ever after, but they do gain an inner comfort, peace, and understanding that they may not have possessed before. On the other hand, those who choose selfishly lose more consistently and thoroughly. Their misdeeds are discovered, and their actions are repaid in full, either through sickness, death, loss, or banishment. In some cases, the results are more complex. The innocent suffer through the mistakes or misdeeds of others, but even if their own lives pay in ways that seem unfair, they gain through spiritual growth.

The importance of moral structure and true innocence

Closely tied to the idea of love is the importance of moral structure. It eventually becomes clear that Mr. Gradgrind naturally assumed a moral structure, though he did not teach it directly. He also had a deep affection for his children, and in his case, his insistence on facts was based on his desire to provide for his children and teach them a sound way of living. What he took for granted, though, did not come through sufficiently in his teaching and thus resulted in such emotional and moral monstrosities as Bitzer and young Tom Gradgrind, Mr. Gradgrind's own son. Mr. Harthouse was another example of this lack of moral structure, and the destructiveness and inadequacy of his philosophy was clearly demonstrated in its awful effect on Louisa and on Harthouse's inability to resist the loving and truthful demands of Sissy Jupe, a true innocent.

The importance of wonder and imagination

Another element in the human makeup that was ignored by the philosophy of facts was the need for wonder, imagination, and amusement. The symbol of this was the traveling horseback-riding show, which excited the children's curiosity early on but which was forbidden by their father. The analogy of sparks flying, in both the hearth and the chimneys, was another way of portraying the smoldering fire of imagination that lay buried in a soul such as Louisa's. Mr. Sleary, the horseback riders' ringleader, thoroughly understood this human love of enjoyment and wonder. He knew that it was not a frivolous side issue but a deep need in the human psyche that also demanded fulfillment and release.

The precariousness of lies

Another of the major themes in *Hard Times* is the idea that inadequate philosophies and lies, to sustain themselves, need to be built upon more lies and half-truths. Mr. Bounderby was the worst case of this. His entire life and success were built on outright lies that he trumpeted to the rest of Coketown on a regular basis. His lies were all-encompassing: they included both his own history and his concepts of others. Tom Gradgrind and Mrs. Sparsit were close runners-up in the lying game. Tom had to cover his tracks in order to steal, and Mrs. Sparsit spent most of her energy either keeping up her aristocratic sense of self or tearing down anyone who got in the way. Mr. Harthouse was slightly more complex. The fundamental inadequacy of his beliefs and lifestyle became evident when finally confronted by true innocence, but he was so thoroughly steeped in them that if he ever possessed any natural innocence or moral sense, it now no longer existed.

The power of mercy and forgiveness

The power of mercy and forgiveness is one of the most profound themes in *Hard Times.* You might view it as the power of love amplified. Mercy and forgiveness imply that there is some obstacle to the normal (or human) expression of love. To be merciful and to forgive despite trying circumstances is to rise above the merely human to the Divine. The two outstanding examples of this are Old Stephen and Rachael, who despite their hard lives retain a gentleness, kindness, and forbearance that exceed ordinary expectations. Stephen even managed to forgive from the depths of an excruciating pain that ultimately resulted in his death, and for this he received heavenly peace and glory. Of all the residents of Coketown, Rachael was the only one who took pity on Stephen's wretched wife, a hopeless, insane alcoholic. On a lesser, more human scale was the forgiveness of Mr. Gradgrind and his daughter Louisa of young Tom Gradgrind, who had grown so far from normal human love and truthfulness that the only approach left was forgiveness. But it was a forgiveness that stemmed from genuine love—and therein lay its power to ultimately change his mind.

Characters

Mr. Thomas Gradgrind

One of Coketown's leading citizens and the principal of the school, Mr. Thomas Gradgrind is a die-hard "fact" man when we first meet him. His philosophy contains no room for useless nonsense, and he is determined to educate all of Coketown's children by this philosophy. His own five children, trained in all sorts of "-ologies," appear to be models of this system—until things begin to fall apart. But Mr. Gradgrind is not devoid of fatherly affection or moral conviction, and when he sees the ultimately damaging outcomes brought about by his methods, he proves to be a humane man capable of change and growth.

Louisa Gradgrind Bounderby

If there is a central character in *Hard Times,* it is probably Louisa Gradgrind, Mr. Gradgrind's eldest child and daughter. She is also his pride and joy, the proof that his system brings positive results. But unbeknownst to Gradgrind and, to some extent, to Louisa herself, these results were at her expense, yet it's only later that this becomes obvious. One of the early metaphors in the novel is the hearth fire. In between learning her various –ologies, Louisa would sit and stare at the fire, noticing the sparks as they suddenly burst forth and then died. A similar imagery existed in Coketown's smokestacks, which, monotonous and gray during the daytime, would emit bursts of flame at night. These fiery bursts made her think of how short and precious life was. But they also symbolized the flame of imagination and wonder that struggled to burst forth from the layers and layers of tyrannical fact-training that had nearly choked them out of existence. More than any other character in the story, Louisa embodies this idea, and it comes to its full head after her unsatisfying marriage to Josiah Bounderby is threatened by the advances of James Harthouse. Louisa is too disciplined and goodhearted to succumb, but the inner war triggered by the strain of the situation is too much for her, and she nearly snaps. That weakness, though, proves to be a turning point for the Gradgrind family, whose various members are now forced to confront the system that brought them to that point and, in the best cases, to adopt a more humane and human approach.

Sissy Jupe

Just as Louisa embodies the struggle between systems, Sissy Jupe presents the clearest idea of pure innocence, mercy, and love. She seems to know nothing of vengeance, doubt, or pride—from the time she first appears on the scene as the abandoned daughter of the circus horseback rider to her pivotal role in the fate of the Gradgrind family and, ultimately, many other lives. Though sorely lacking in the facts department, she more than makes up for it by her humanity, caring, and faith. She never loses hope that her father will return someday (though he dies in the end) or that love and faith, coupled with the best human efforts, can triumph over any challenge.

Tom Gradgrind ("The Whelp")

Nicknamed "the whelp" by Dickens because of his wolflike qualities, young Tom Gradgrind was nothing like his father, though he was to some extent the product of his father's system. Whatever the fact-based system did not teach about moral structure or spiritual culture, young Tom dutifully neglected to learn. Nourished by his sister's love, he managed to subsist on his own spiritual and emotional barrenness until he was later robbed of her presence—but by then it was too late. His claim to fame was that he stole from the Coketown bank owned by Mr. Bounderby, Louisa's husband, and then blamed an innocent worker, Stephen Blackpool, who later died because of the incident. His carelessness and villainy were among the strongest challenges to the Gradgrind system and the catalyst for another turning point in the elder Thomas Gradgrind's philosophy.

Mrs. Gradgrind

Mrs. Gradgrind is an important minor character, the earliest demonstration of the sickliness and weakness that happen to mind and body when crucial aspects of the human being are suppressed. Sissy Jupe's presence in her life (for Sissy never managed to learn her facts adequately, so she was relegated to helping Mrs. Gradgrind) was a significant benefit. Sissy's ability to express love enabled Mrs. Gradgrind to catch a glimpse of something that was missing from the Gradgrind philosophy an idea that she struggled to express immediately before her death.

Mr. Josiah Bounderby of Coketown

One of *Hard Times'* most inflated, egotistical characters is Mr. Josiah Bounderby, or "Josiah Bounderby of Coketown," as he liked to call himself. A good friend of Mr. Gradgrind and a propounder of the facts philosophy, Bounderby epitomizes one of the philosophy's worst characteristics: self-interest. He is one of the wealthiest of Coketown's citizens, a self-made man who owns several businesses and has no qualms about the fact that his success was built on the sweating backs of his overworked employees. His own life supposedly began in penury, something he liked to brag about endlessly. Presumably abandoned by his wretched mother as an infant, he was raised by his even more wretched, alcoholic grandmother, who kept him in an egg box. From there, he landed in the gutter until he finally scratched his way up to the remarkable self-made man that he was. All of these woeful tales turned out to be lies that eventually blew up in Bounderby's face: his marriage to Louisa, which never flourished, fell apart; his relationship with his housekeeper blew up; his bank was robbed by his own apprentice, and out of arrogance, he terminated his relationship with his best friend, Mr. Gradgrind. In the end, he died an early death and was replaced by future versions of himself.

Mrs. Sparsit

Mrs. Sparsit's extraordinary claim to fame is her aristocratic background. As Mr. Bounderby's housekeeper, she is acutely aware of her lowered station in life due to marital misfortune and an uncomfortable relationship with her aunt, Lady Scadgers. But she makes the most of her situation, and until Mr. Bounderby's marriage to Louisa, which effectively supplants Mrs. Sparsit as the female head of the Bounderby household, they mutually support each other by feeding each other's self-esteem.

Louisa's arrival, however, is too much for Mrs. Sparsit, and it quickly brings out her worst characteristics. She turns into a petty, vindictive busybody, who makes several poor judgment calls that end up having multiple destructive effects. She is ultimately terminated from her position and forced to scrape out a difficult and unpleasant existence with her aunt. However, by the time Bounderby terminates her, she has come to despise him so thoroughly that she treats the event more like a triumph than a loss.

Mr. Sleary

Mr. Sleary (or "Thleary," in this own wordth, thinth he talkth with a lithp) is one of the novel's most colorful characters. The leader of the traveling horse-riding show, which is similar to a circus, he is the antithesis of the fact men. Warm and funny, and never without his brandy and water, Mr. Sleary has an intuitive sense of what makes human beings happy, and though he doesn't draw between the lines in terms of "proper" behavior, he has a good heart and a healthy dose of common sense and humanity. Forever grateful to Thomas Gradgrind for taking in Sissy Jupe in her time of need (Sissy's father worked for Sleary), he comes through with the equivalent gesture when Gradgrind desperately attempts to save his wayward son. Towards the end of the novel, Dickens uses him as the mouthpiece for one of the most profound statements in the book. That scene in itself, in which Sleary, brandy in hand, speaks of the deepest universal wisdom, is the novel's exemplification of the idea that the truth can never be judged by externals. He later repeats this idea to Gradgrind when he reminds him that, no matter how the horse riders might appear, they have their place in the world, and he should make the best and not the worst of them.

"Old Stephen" Blackpool

Stephen Blackpool, or "Old Stephen," is one of the "Hands," the working-class folk who in this case manned the looms. Back in Dickens's time, an ordinary adult workday was fifteen hours, and in Coketown's weaving mills that meant fifteen hours surrounded by endless noise and motion. Yet Stephen, who is a deep believer in Christianity, bears it all with a saintly patience and gentleness and, for the most part, not a shred of resentment for his hard and simple lot in life. Occasionally, he is visited by his wretched wife, a hopeless drunk who has lost her mind, and that places a strain on him. But Stephen has an angel in his life, Rachael, and Rachael is his saving grace. Unfortunately, his problems don't end with his estranged wife, nor can his life be salvaged by Rachael. He is unjustly accused of treachery and selfishness by his co-workers on the one hand and his master on the other, with the result that he is forced to leave town to live and seek work elsewhere. Out of compassion, Louisa secretly visits his apartment to help by offering him some money. He only accepts a little, with the intention of paying it back.

Had things ended there, it would have been a lovely gesture on both parts; but Louisa brought Tom along, and Tom, already in a desperate state of his own, took Stephen aside in private and talked him into waiting outside the bank for the next few evenings, without saying why. Innocently, Stephen agreed, not knowing that Tom intended to use him as a decoy. Tom never showed up to meet him, and once the robbery was accomplished, Stephen was accused of the crime. By the time of the robbery, though, he had already been gone for two days. Rachael sent him a letter to summon him back to clear his name, but Stephen never showed.

The whole affair turns into a general mystery until Rachael and Sissy take the train to the country one Sunday to get some fresh air. Sissy accidentally discovers a deep pit, the Old Hell Shaft. It turns out that Stephen fell into it the night he set out to Bounderby's country home to clear his name after receiving the letter. The people from the surrounding countryside are gathered together to form a rescue party, and Stephen's weakened, crumpled body is retrieved from the shaft. Down in the pit, alone and in pain, one star seemed to especially shine down on Old Stephen. To him, it symbolized the Star of Bethlehem, the Guiding Light, and its light transformed his thoughts from consternation and anger to faith and forgiveness. He died as the rescue party carried him away on the litter, with his beloved Rachael holding his hand and the Guiding Star of his life shining down upon him.

Rachael

Rachael is Stephen's female friend and counterpart in simplicity, goodness, and gentleness. They loved each other deeply and often walked home together, but that was the extent of their physical interaction.

Had Stephen been free of his marriage, which happened long ago and then went bad, he would have married Rachael. As friends, they were deeply faithful to each other. The night Stephen's wife showed up at his apartment, drunk and insane, Stephen arrived home to find Rachael tending her by his bedside. When he had nightmares and thoughts of murder, Rachael's goodness inspired him and saved him from himself, prompting him to kneel down before her and call her his Angel. After Stephen was accused, Rachael was the one who sought to vindicate him. And when Stephen's poor body was brought up from the pit, it was Rachael's face looking down on him and Rachael who held his hand in hers until the moment of his death.

Mr. James Harthouse

Mr. James Harthouse is a perfect example of the quintessential jaded, lackadaisical, utterly amoral English gentleman. In that respect, he is the antithesis of Josiah Bounderby, whose inflated blustering does not read well against Harthouse's elegant manners. Through his brother's connections, Harthouse signs on as a business associate with the fact men of Coketown and then comes to live at the Bounderby country estate. Fascinated by Louisa, he cannot fathom her mysterious, disciplined demeanor. He challenges himself to win her trust and affection, which he succeeds in doing by studying her psychology and capitalizing on her relationships, good and bad. In the process, he falls in love with her, and when Bounderby is out of town one stormy night, he rides to the estate to be with her. She repels him, however, forcing him to leave. Desperate, upset, and contending with violently conflicting feelings, she flees to her father's house, where she reveals everything to him and then, faint and distraught, drops down onto the floor. When Louisa awakens, she is visited by Sissy, who gains her trust and then takes the situation with Harthouse into her own hands. Harthouse is still in a frenzy over Louisa, and when Sissy unexpectedly shows up at his hotel room, he is unprepared for the power of her innocence, rectitude, and love. Her self-appointed mission is to free Louisa of his troubling company, and she gently but firmly orders him to permanently leave town. Floored by her presence, he finds himself unable to resist her command, and so, having made all necessary communications, he immediately packs up and leaves for Egypt.

Mrs. Pegler

Mrs. Pegler is the mysterious elderly lady who periodically appears in Coketown to hover around Bounderby's estate, waiting for the great master of Coketown to emerge so that she can catch a glimpse of him. She usually latches onto some unsuspecting Hand who happens to be walking by. In several cases, it was Stephen; in another, Rachael. The night that Louisa visited Stephen's apartment, Mrs. Pegler happened to be there, having been invited for tea. Afraid of being seen by Louisa, she tried to hide in shadows, but Louisa noticed her anyway. That incident, which was later revealed through questioning, implicated Mrs. Pegler in the bank robbery. That, in turn, got Mrs. Sparsit's juices flowing, and she went on a search that ended in her dragging the poor elderly lady back to Coketown by train. Having dragged her out of the train, Mrs. Sparsit brought her to Bounderby's Coketown home (as opposed to the country estate, which had been put up for sale after the Bounderby marriage fell apart). They were followed by about twenty-five random spectators, who gathered in the dining room. It turned out that the poor lady was Mr. Bounderby's mother; that none of the ridiculous childhood stories he had told were true; that his parents and grandmother had been kind, self-sacrificing, respectable people who gave Josiah every opportunity; and that Bounderby had paid his mother to be quiet. In her kindness and innocence, she never grasped the fraudulent nature of her son's behavior but remained proud of his accomplishments to the last.

Chapter Summaries

BOOK I—SOWING

Chapter 1—The One Thing Needful

Facts, facts, facts—Chapter 1 of Book 1 (*Sowing*) portrays an unidentified man emphatically telling the schoolmaster to teach the children nothing but facts. Dickens describes in detail how his uncompromising overall look underscores his speech: his square forehead, deep-set eyes, knobby balding head, thin lips, dry yet overbearing voice, and otherwise square, rigid appearance all illustrate his stubborn, dogmatic attitude. Watching him deliver his speech were the schoolmaster, another unidentified adult, and a classroom full of schoolchildren who awaited the outpouring of facts they were about to receive. Dickens, of course, presents all of this in a much more colorful manner.

Chapter 2—Murdering the Innocents

Sissy Jupe's introduction to the hard facts philosophy—The name of the man in question is Thomas Gradgrind, known for his love of calculation and hard facts. His first unfortunate target among the roomful of innocent schoolchildren was a girl named Sissy Jupe, whom he addressed as "girl number twenty" as he asked her to identify herself. When she told him her name, he informed her that the name Sissy was not good enough, insisting that she call herself Cecilia from now on, even though her father called her Sissy. He likewise turned his nose up at her father's profession, so he renamed it: instead of a horseback rider, her father was to be referred to as a veterinarian, farrier,[1] and horse trainer. When he asked her to define a horse, she was at a complete loss.

Bitzer gives a factual description of a horse—Appalled at her lack of horse facts, Mr. Gradgrind instead called on a young boy named Bitzer, who happened to be illuminated by the same ray of sunshine that had made Sissy stand out. Here, Dickens describes the division in the schoolroom of boys on one side and girls on the other. Bitzer, whose pale complexion contrasted with Sissy's dark-brown hair and eyes, gave Mr. Gradgrind a factual, scientific answer that described a horse's exact number and type of teeth along with the scientific names for what it ate, how many legs it had, and so on. Pleased, Mr. Gradgrind informed "girl number twenty" that she now knew what a horse was. Deeply embarrassed, Sissy curtseyed out of respect for Mr. Gradgrind, and both children sat down.

Taste is defined by facts—Next Dickens introduces the third anonymous adult, a government agent who, by his own account, was a boxer, both literally and figuratively in the sense that the same boxing attitude colored his overall approach. His question to the pupils was whether they would paper the room with horse drawings. To this he got a divided response because, as usual, half the room waited to see the man's reaction to what the first half said. As it turned out, "no" was the right answer, the reason being that horses never walked up walls; therefore, their pictures should never be displayed on walls. Taste, he insisted, was to be defined by fact: whatever was not factual was lacking in taste.

His next question along the same lines was whether the children would carpet the room with pictures of flowers. Convinced by now that "no" was usually the correct answer, most of them shouted "no." However, a few brave souls eked out a meager "yes," among them, Sissy Jupe. When the anonymous

---

[1] Someone who shoes horses

gentleman saw that, he called upon her to explain herself. She simply told him that she liked flowers, to which he replied that to like ("fancy") something was not factual and that she should strike that word from her vocabulary. He repeated that whatever did not happen, in fact, should not be represented in any way. If, for example, people did not walk on flowers or allow butterflies to sit on their dishes, or if horses did not walk up walls, then these things should never be portrayed anywhere else. Everything, he stressed again, was to be mathematical and factual. Thoroughly intimidated, Sissy sat back down.

Mr. M'Choakumchild, the schoolmaster—Finally, the two men called on the schoolmaster, Mr. M'Choakumchild, to demonstrate his teaching method. Mr. M'Choakumchild, along with 140 other schoolteachers, had been thoroughly trained in the knowledge of facts as they pertained to a host of subjects, from grammar and spelling to science and even voice lessons. The question in Dickens's mind was whether all that learning truly enhanced Mr. M'Choakumchild's teaching ability or whether a little less learning might have made him a better teacher. He ends the chapter wondering whether this flood of learning would ultimately choke the children's imaginations.

Chapter 3—A Loophole

Mr. Thomas Gradgrind, Coketown's school principal—In Chapter 3, we discover that Thomas Gradgrind is the principal of the school and, therefore, determined to be a model of factualness for the children. His own five children had been trained to be models since the time they were young, which means that they were exposed only to facts and prevented from learning anything imaginative. Their image of a cow or a constellation was similar to Bitzer's description of a horse—dry, factual, scientific. No poetry, no children's stories … nothing that would excite the imagination was allowed.

Stone Lodge—As Chapter 3 opens, Mr. Gradgrind is on his way to Stone Lodge, his home on the moor, no more than two miles outside of Coketown, the area's large town. Gradgrind's current goal in life is to become a member a Parliament. Having previously worked in the hardware wholesale business, he built Stone Lodge after his retirement. Dickens describes Stone Lodge as a well-calculated house with all the modern amenities: numerous windows symmetrically arranged on either side; water, plumbing, ventilation, fireproofing, and gas; a garden and lawn with a toddler's walkway ("infant avenue"); and elevators for the household help. The children's practical education was also well provided for. They had cabinets dedicated to various types of scientific specimens, including mollusk shells, metals, and minerals.

Sleary's Horse-Riding show—Though Gradgrind was affectionate toward his children, his great pride in life was to be considered "eminently practical." This was how he saw himself, and it was how he liked to be seen. As Gradgrind reached the town's edge, his self-satisfied musings were interrupted by the band music wafting over from the horse-riding ring where Sissy's father worked. "Sleary's Horse-Riding" it was called, and it was currently hosting a performance featuring Miss Josephine Sleary on horseback in her Tyrolean flower act and Mr. Jupe himself, with his trained dog Merrylegs, his rapid-fire iron weight-throwing act, his Shakespearean quotes, and his comic horseback depiction of Mr. William Button in *The Tailor's Journey to Brentford.*

Gradgrind catches his own children peeking—Determined to ignore such frivolousness, Mr. Gradgrind continued walking. As he passed by the back, though, he noticed a group of children kneeling down and peeking into the ring through a hole as they tried to catch a glimpse of the flower act. It occurred to him to look more closely so that he might deter any schoolchildren he recognized from wasting their valuable time. To his horrified amazement, he saw two of his own children, Louisa and Thomas, straining to see the show. Mr. Gradgrind wasted no time in walking over to them, placing his hands upon them, and authoritatively exclaiming their names. Embarrassed, they stood up as they were asked to explain themselves. They were curious, they both admitted, again to their father's astonishment. He could not understand how they, who were loaded with scientific facts and trained to be mathematically precise, could possibly stoop so low—both literally and figuratively—that they would peek through a hole into a horseback-riding ring!

Louisa Gradgrind—Gradgrind soon discovered, contrary to his expectations, that Louisa had brought Thomas to the ring. Louisa was around fifteen, and the fact that she was about to become a woman had not escaped her father. Neither had her natural willfulness, which had been tempered by her upbringing. She had been thoroughly trained to be dry and factual, yet in spite of this, Dickens describes a light within her that struggled to find its way to the surface—flashes of imagination that yearned for a fuller expression. Now, as her father led them home, both their faces betrayed the sense of hopeless entrapment they felt.

What would Mr. Bounderby think?—Louisa, however, was direct about her feelings. She explained to her father that she had been tired for a long time, though she couldn't say exactly why. Her father was too intolerant of the idea to listen further and instead tried to shame her with what her best friends would think—or Mr. Bounderby? He repeated the question over and over again, and the mention of Bounderby's name caught Louisa's attention as she stole a searching glance in her father's direction, something he totally missed. He was too busy shaming his two unhappy children as he led them home.

Chapter 4—Mr. Bounderby

Mr. Josiah Bounderby of Coketown—In Chapter 4, we meet Mr. Josiah Bounderby himself, a large, coarse, self-made man, who was fond of boasting that he had pulled himself up by the bootstraps (if he'd had any). For Mr. Bounderby had been a vagabond—or what we now call a homeless person—in his young years, and through sheer grit and determination, he had worked his way up in the world to become one the leading figures of Coketown, with businesses that included banking, manufacturing, and retail.

Mr. Bounderby's appearance betrayed his background somewhat, being the opposite of refined. Everything about him bulged. His head, the veins in his forehead, in fact, his whole being seemed puffed up, possibly from his constant boasting with his brassy voice about how far he had come in life. What hair he still had on his balding head was perpetually unkempt, with a wind-blown look that Dickens likens to a haystack, and though he was slightly younger than Mr. Gradgrind, he looked older.

Bounderby at Stone Lodge, boasting to Mrs. Gradgrind—Dickens describes his relationship with Mr. Gradgrind as being the closest thing to best friend as two dry, factual men could get, so it's no surprise when we find Mr. Bounderby conversing with Mrs. Gradgrind in the drawing room of Stone Lodge. Mrs. Gradgrind was the opposite of Mr. Bounderby in appearance and conduct—thin, frail, sickly, and weak. She was also dry and factual in her way, but she seemed constantly on the verge of fainting in response to some unpleasant fact. That day, as he stood in front of the fireplace in the damp house, Bounderby entertained Mrs. Gradgrind with the story of his rugged youth; his mother's abandonment of him when he was an infant; his drunken grandmother, who kept him in an egg box; how he ran away from home as soon as he could; how he lived in ditches as a vagabond—by his own assessment, a pest and a burden on society; and finally, how, even without an education, he gradually raised himself up and out of his poor, sickly condition to his current impressive status as a wealthy and influential citizen.

Just as Bounderby was finishing his speech, Mr. Gradgrind entered with his two guilty children in tow. Dickens is explicit about how Bounderby asked about Thomas's sullen expression while simultaneously looking at Louisa. Without looking up and without apology, Louisa admitted that their father caught them sneaking a peak at the circus. Mortified, their mother immediately began scolding them and finally sent them to their room to do "somethingological." Mrs. Gradgrind herself did not have much of a head for "somethingological" facts. Yet Gradgrind had found her a good prospect because of her utter lack of imagination, or "nonsense," as he termed it.

Gradgrind questions the source of his children's waywardness—The children having repaired to their room, Gradgrind sought Bounderby's advice on this most disturbing issue, namely, that his children seemed to have developed an unintended mental quality. Somehow it had managed to squeeze itself in among all those facts, and Gradgrind could not fathom its source. "Idle imagination," offered Bounderby without hesitation. Still mystified, Gradgrind continued trying to pinpoint the external source that might have caused this wayward interest in his children. Was it a servant or a teacher? Maybe something the children had read? It simply didn't make sense, given their straight-laced, factual upbringing.

Sissy Jupe suspected as the catalyst—Suddenly, the lightbulb went on in Bounderby's head. Wasn't the new girl at school the offspring of one of the circus people? Unhappily, Gradgrind admitted that she had personally applied at the house for admission to the school and that Louisa had seen her, though certainly, he thought, in Mrs. Gradgrind's presence. Bounderby, again without hesitation, proclaimed that the solution was to immediately turn the girl around. Gradgrind agreed, so they set off together toward the town and Sissy Jupe's home.

Bounderby looks in on the children and asks Louisa for a kiss—While Bounderby waited in the hall for Gradgrind to retrieve the address, he decided to poke his head into the children's study. Dickens's describes the room as having the atmosphere of a hair-cutting room, in spite of all the "somethingological" materials it held. Except for the two youngest boys, who were being lectured somewhere else, the children were all relatively idle: the youngest, Jane, with pipe clay smeared all over her face, was sleeping, having dozed off while studying fractions. Thomas was sitting by the fire, and Louisa was looking out the window. Bounderby consoled Thomas and Louisa, saying that everything was all right now, and then he asked Louisa whether that wasn't worth a kiss. Reluctantly and without affection, she went over to him and offered her cheek. After he left, she spent more than five minutes rubbing the spot where he had kissed her, which prompted her brother to remark that she was likely to rub a hole in her face. Thoroughly disgusted, she replied that she wouldn't cry even if he cut the spot out with a pocketknife.

Chapter 5—The Key-note

Coketown—Chapter 5 starts with a description of Coketown, a town that was as grim and factual as its leading citizens. Mostly built of brick smeared with soot, Coketown had a red and black appearance. The soot came from the factory chimneys, which belched endless trails of smoke. Even the canal was black, and the town's river was darkened and foul-smelling with dye from the factories, which generated a humdrum noise and shaking throughout the day.

Coketown's streets, whether large or small, had a sameness about them. Its buildings looked the same regardless of their function, which was their main distinction. The same was true of the town's eighteen churches, which, except for one stucco building, were built of brick and mostly unornamented. Most of its inhabitants, too, led dull, repetitive lives, going to the same factory jobs at the same time, year in and year out. In short, it was an entirely practical, financially expedient town.

Pastimes of Coketown's workers—Coketown, however, was not without its mysteries. One of these was the question of who actually attended all those churches since the working people apparently had better things to do. They remained firmly planted in their homes, where instead of listening to the Word of God, they proceeded to get drunk or take opium—much to the dismay of various town groups, such as the religious fanatics, the Teetotal Society, and the pharmacists and chemists. Matters got even worse when, according to the jail chaplain, these same people would gather in lowbrow places, where they would engage in vulgar singing and watch (and maybe even participate in) vulgar dancing. Not only that, according to the two factual, practical gentlemen, Bounderby and Gradgrind, these same people were never satisfied despite their preference for the best meat, fresh butter, and mocha coffee. Dickens wonders whether their malaise didn't have its roots in the same source as the unhappy spirits of the Gradgrind children. Perhaps their imaginations had been squashed for too long and were seeking a way out—some mode of expression to bring a little joy and color to their lives.

Gradgrind and Bounderby meet Sissy Jupe—As Gradgrind and Bounderby paused while deciding which way to go next, Sissy Jupe came dashing madly around the corner. When Gradgrind called to her to stop and explain herself, she told him that she was being chased and was trying to get away. At that moment, Bitzer came running at such high speed that he charged right into Mr. Gradgrind. Whatever the real story was, Bitzer was ready with an answer that played on the girl's inferior social status and the poor reputation of circus riders, who were considered unreliable and even dishonest. After sending him away, Gradgrind instructed Sissy to lead them to her father's home. Noticing a bottle in her hand, he questioned her about it and discovered that (contrary to Bounderby's opinion that it was gin) it contained nine oils for rubbing the bruises her father had acquired in the ring. Bounderby went on about how it served them right and how, in his younger days he had been even more severely bruised by whipping, but Gradgrind took a kinder tone. As they entered Pod's End, they approached the small, old, worn-out pub that was Sissy's home. The girl warned them of Merrylegs' bark and asked them to wait while she fetched a candle. On entering the pub, Bounderby laughed with what Dickens describes as his "metallic" laugh: for a self-made man like him to be dealing with nine oils and a dog named Merrylegs seemed terribly ironic.

Chapter 6—Sleary's Horsemanship

Pegasus's Arms—With evening descending over the town, it was already too dark outside to see the sign above the door that announced the name of the pub as Pegasus's Arms. The sign depicted Pegasus, the winged horse of Greek mythology, with four verses beneath it announcing the availability of good liquor inside—probably too fanciful a sign for the likes of Gradgrind and Bounderby. Inside, it was also dark, which was just as well, since another even more fanciful and vulgar depiction of Pegasus—complete with gold stars, gauze, and red silk—graced the wall over the bar.

Sissy's father missing—When Sissy discovered that her father was not there, she invited the gentlemen to sit in the dingy little room while she went looking for him. Except for a white cap with peacock feathers and a pigtail that Mr. Jupe wore in his Shakespeare performances, there was no sign of either him or the dog. The men could hear Sissy looking through different rooms and talking to people, and presently she reappeared in a panic. After looking in an old trunk that turned out to be empty, she concluded—though it didn't make sense—that he must be down at the ring. She promised to return "in a minute" as she hurriedly left.

E. W. B. Childers and Master Kidderminster—Gradgrind, who took her literally, was trying to figure out how she could make it back that quickly. His thoughts were interrupted by the appearance of a young man whom Dickens describes as having a thin, sallow face, a heap of dark hair, disproportionately short strong legs, and an equally disproportionate, broad torso. The man looked and smelled like a combination of the theater and the stable, and by his side stood a young lad, described by Dickens as a "child with an old face," who was dressed to look like Cupid and had his face covered with white and red makeup. These two, Mr. E. W. B. Childers and Master Kidderminster, had a jumping act called the Wild Huntsman, in which Childers held the diminutive Kidderminster upside down.

Mr. Childers began the conversation by asking whether Gradgrind and Bounderby were the two gentlemen who had been looking for Mr. Jupe. Mr. Gradgrind confirmed the question but quickly added that they had no time to wait and would, therefore, like to leave him a message. Mr. Bounderby felt compelled to distinguish himself and Mr. Gradgrind as from that class of people who knew the value of time, unlike those whom they addressed. Without missing a beat, Mr. Childers agreed that if he was referring to the use of time as earning power, then his appearance suggested he must be right. At this point, Master Kidderminster, who looked angelic in performance, revealed himself to be rude and ornery in person. He added that Bounderby probably knew how to keep his money as well, complaining that if he had come to give them a hard time, he should pay his entrance fee and do so in the ring. In response to both these comments, Childers quickly instructed him to keep quiet.

Mr. Jupe's decline as a performer—As the conversation progressed, it emerged that Mr. Jupe's abilities had declined lately, to the point that he had been booed a number of times, most recently in the presence of his daughter. This was a greater shame to him than the event itself. Childers's assessment was that Jupe no longer had his former strength and flexibility and was, therefore, regularly botching his act. This message was delivered with so much circus lingo that Gradgrind had to ask for an interpretation several times. Childers's conclusion with regard to Jupe was that he was not likely to return and that a message would be wasted.

In his usual self-engrossed way, Bounderby took the opportunity to relate Mr. Jupe's desertion of his daughter to his own sorry background and his resentment of his mother for doing the same to him. That background, he insisted, had made him the factual and unsentimental man he now was. Therefore, he could proclaim without hesitation that, like his own mother, Mr. Jupe was obviously a scoundrel and a drifter. To that, Childers retorted that whatever names people assigned to Jupe were irrelevant to him and that Mr. Bounderby should keep his opinions to himself while there and instead express them in his own buildings. Bounderby's laugh indicated that he was not particularly perturbed by the comment, but he complied.

Childers suggests Gradgrind take in Sissy—Mr. Childers then turned to Mr. Gradgrind to explain the situation further, namely, that he had seen Jupe slipping out with a small bundle after sending Sissy on an errand. Childers was concerned that Sissy would have a difficult time accepting her father's disappearance because she and her father had been so close. He lamented that she might have been better off if her father had apprenticed her to the circus. Instead, his goal was to get her an education, so he was thrilled when she was accepted into the school—though Childers couldn't figure out why, since his work required a transient lifestyle. But things now being as they were, Childers entertained the vague hope that Gradgrind would take Sissy under his wing. As it happened, Gradgrind had originally come to expel her from the school, with the conviction that her father's trade made her unsuitable for that environment, but under the present circumstances, he could see that another approach might be in order, so he asked Mr. Childers to give him a moment to confer privately with Mr. Bounderby.

The riding troupe gathers—As Mr. Childers waited outside the room, the rest of the riding troupe slowly appeared from their upstairs lodgings and before long had entered the room where Mr. Gradgrind and Mr. Bounderby were conferring. There were about twenty of them all together, including men, women, children, and grandmothers, and though they were relatively rough and unschooled, they had an air of innocence and kindness. All of them had some sort of balancing, twirling, juggling, tightrope walking, or riding talent, but none of them spent much time on either personal appearance or housework.

Mr. Sleary—Finally, there was the ringmaster himself, Mr. Sleary, a corpulent man with a wandering eye, who spoke with a lisp and a voice that barely worked anymore from overexposure to changing temperatures as a youth in the ring. Addressing Mr. Gradgrind as "Thquire" in his perpetually half-drunk, half-sober manner, Mr. Sleary inquired whether Gradgrind had any special plans to help Miss Jupe, given that her father had disappeared. Pleased to hear that Gradgrind had a proposal for her when she returned, he added that he, too, would offer her the option of an apprenticeship with his riding company, even though she would be starting later than most trainees.

Sissy decides to go with Mr. Gradgrind—At that point, Sissy burst into the room and began wailing in despair when she saw everyone gathered and her father still missing. One of the women comforted her, taking the girl in her arms as they both knelt on the floor, but Sissy continued bemoaning her beloved father, whom she was sure had left to do some kindness for her. After a bit of this, Bounderby felt compelled to emphasize the now done fact of Mr. Jupe's disappearance, relating it—as always—to his own background. Unimpressed by his lack of empathy, the horse riders were visibly offended, prompting Mr. Sleary to issue Bounderby a warning that if he kept it up, he was liable be tossed out the window. With Bounderby now quiet, Mr. Gradgrind made his proposal: whereas he had originally intended to oust Sissy from the school because of her father's occupation, under the current conditions, with her father obviously missing, he was willing to take her in and educate her, provided she had nothing more to do with her current group of acquaintances. After Sleary put forward his offer of apprenticeship and what she stood to gain from it, Gradgrind stressed the benefits of an education and his understanding that it would have been her father's wish. This last point got the girl's attention so suddenly and fully that the whole room knew in that moment that she had decided to go with Gradgrind. Seeing her sudden conviction, Gradgrind warned her to make sure she that she had a full awareness of her own thoughts on the matter. When she voiced her concern over how her father would find her if he did reappear, Gradgrind assured her that he was well known and, therefore, easy to find. Furthermore, he would have no right to prevent her from going back to her father. After another moment of pondering, Sissy again burst into tears and cried out to the others to gather up her clothes before her heart broke altogether. As the women mournfully collected her few bits of clothing into a basket, Sissy sat on the floor and wept while the men watched from the center of the room—that is all except Bounderby and Gradgrind, who waited by the door.

Sissy says goodbye; Sleary's parting advice—Having said all her goodbyes and hugged everyone in the room (except Master Kidderminster, who had an aversion to such things), she finally came to Sleary. After giving her his blessing and an affectionate kiss, Mr. Sleary handed Sissy over to Mr. Gradgrind. Reminding her to abide by her agreement, he told her to follow Mr. Gradgrind's rules and forget her horse-riding friends. But, Sleary added, if ever she should happen upon them as a grown, well-to-do married woman, hopefully she would find it in her heart to not disdain them but to be generous toward them. Turning to Gradgrind, he added that people could not spend their entire lives in drudgery or education—they needed some sort of amusement to brighten their day—and, therefore, to think of entertainers in their best and not their worst light.

Chapter 7—Mrs. Sparsit

Mrs. Sparsit's aristocratic background—Mr. Bounderby's housekeeper was the elderly Mrs. Sparsit. Mrs. Sparsit was no ordinary housekeeper but had the distinction of an aristocratic background. Her late husband, who died of alcoholism at twenty-four, had been a Powler on his mother's side. The Powlers were an old family, though not the best in terms of family habits, judging from their tendency to lose money at gambling. Sparsit himself had squandered his inheritance so that Mrs. Sparsit was left with nothing.

Mrs. Sparsit takes a job out of need and to spite her aunt, Lady Scadgers—The reason for this unfortunate marriage, which resulted in almost immediate separation, was Mrs. Sparsit's only living relative, Lady Scadgers. Lady Scadgers was Mrs. Sparsit's aunt on her father's side, and it was she who arranged the marriage early on. Dickens describes her as being hugely overweight and unable to get out of bed because of a bad leg. She and her niece were not on good terms, so when Mrs. Sparsit took a job, it was partly an act of vengeance toward her aunt, though she also needed to support herself.

Mr. Bounderby makes the most of Mrs. Sparsit's connections—Mr. Bounderby was not too concerned with these niceties. He reveled in the idea that he, a self-made man with a lowly background, had an aristocrat in his employ—and he made the most of it, emphasizing the worst of his background and the best of hers to accentuate the differences and, therefore, the irony of the situation. It was yet another occasion for him to brag.

Bounderby questions Gradgrind's decision to take on Sissy—The morning after Sissy's decision, Mr. Bounderby was not his usual self, which led Mrs. Sparsit to inquire about why he was eating his breakfast so slowly. He responded that he was thinking about Mr. Gradgrind's decision to raise and educate Sissy Jupe, whom he referred to as "the tumbling girl." He was concerned that she would be a bad influence on Louisa, which prompted Mrs. Sparsit to observe that he was like a second father to Mr. Gradgrind's eldest daughter. He replied that that would be truer of her brother Tom since he planned to take him under his wing once the boy was done with his education.

A mutually respectful relationship—It should be mentioned here that Mrs. Sparsit was more than a servant to Mr. Bounderby. She had not been waiting on him during their conversation but taking tea with him, and he insisted on having her treated with the utmost respect. In fact, the conversation now turned to a comparison of their backgrounds—how she had been born into a world of luxury and ease, while he had struggled with hardship and poverty. She had seen the inside of the Italian Opera, while he had slept on the pavement nearby. Despite their different backgrounds, she seemed sympathetic and even interested, describing his experiences as "instructive."

Gradgrind's final decision and Sissy's promise—As they were speaking, the Gradgrinds arrived with Sissy Jupe, who dutifully curtseyed to all the right people, though she failed include Mrs. Sparsit out of confusion. This elicited an indignant response from Mr. Bounderby, who insisted on having Mrs. Sparsit treated with courtesy and respect. Mr. Gradgrind believed it to be a mistake, and Mrs. Sparsit herself was more forgiving, so with the matter being settled, Gradgrind announced to Sissy that he had made his final decision to take her in and educate her. When she was not in school, she would be taking care of Mrs. Gradgrind and she was never to mention her previous life. He then asked her about her former activity of reading to her father and the rest of the riders. She claimed she had only read to her father and that those were the happiest times. When he asked her what she had read him, she said they were tales of genies, fairies, dwarves, and a hunchback. Hearing that, Gradgrind reminded her to never speak of those things again.

An air of dejection—During all this, Louisa kept her eyes on the ground and seemed quite cold, only looking at Sissy when her sadness became obvious. As they walked to Stone Lodge, Louisa said nothing. Dickens ends the chapter with a comment about Mrs. Sparsit, who spent the evening pondering the dejected feeling of their exit.

Chapter 8—Never Wonder

Train them while they're young—One of Mr. Gradgrind's techniques for taming the minds of his young charges was to never allow them to wonder. That was strictly prohibited in favor of some form of calculation—and certainly never any feelings. The best way to accomplish this was to start when they were young, just this side of infancy. Unfortunately, Coketown harbored a great many people who, though their bodies had grown to adulthood, still retained the untrained mental habits of a toddler. Coketown's eighteen religious denominations, despite their other differences, agreed on the importance of retraining this sorry species, who preferred adventure novels to mathematics—sometimes indulging in them even after a fifteen-hour workday.

Young Tom Gradgrind's misery—All the facts and figures finally got the better of young Tom Gradgrind, who now complained to Louisa that he hated his life and everyone around him—except her. His outlook was so dark that he was even convinced that Sissy Jupe hated not just him but all of them, and he had already noticed a distinct change for the worse in her mood and color, which was paler than before. He felt like a donkey, stubborn, stupid, miserable, and wishing he could kick everyone except Louisa. Their home seemed to him more like a jail, and Louisa was the only bright spot. Even if she didn't feel it herself, she had the ability to comfort him.

Louisa's sense that something was missing—That seemed strange to Louisa, who knew that she lacked the knowledge that other girls had. Not the grim, factual knowledge they were all exposed to in that house, but the lighter, more amusing knowledge that seemed to relieve the spirits of those who had it—the ability to sing or play, or to tell compelling stories from life or books. As she sat in her dark corner, watching the fire with her brother, she admitted that it was something she had wondered about many times. One thing was certain for both of them: they were missing something fundamental, and their lives were the worse for it.

Tom's plans to manipulate Bounderby—Tom wished he could take all the facts and figures he'd ever learned, including all the people who had discovered them, and blow them up in one big blast. But soon, he felt, he would have his revenge. He would have more freedom, he thought, when staying with Mr. Bounderby. Louisa warned him that Bounderby was even harsher and far less kind than their father, but Tom was convinced he would know how to handle him. When asked how he would manage to do that, he replied that his secret weapon was her: he would use Bounderby's love of her to manipulate him.

Louisa's fascination with the fire—To this she said nothing, which prompted Tom to ask if she had fallen asleep. She replied that she was watching the fire. He noticed that she seemed to see more in it than he ever could, probably, he thought because she was a girl. In fact, Dickens makes a number of allusions throughout the book to some subtle quality in Louisa, some spark of imagination that had a positive effect on others, though some—like Bounderby—didn't necessarily know why. Even she was only partially aware of it and perceived it more as a lack than as a present quality.

Louisa wonders about their future—At least, Tom added, he would be getting away from home, though he regretted leaving her, both for his own sake and hers. He asked her whether she understood the value of having her as form of leverage. Louisa finally answered yes, but it took her so long that he went over to her chair and stood behind it to see what she was seeing in the fire. Unable to figure it out, he asked her directly, but she replied that she saw nothing. However, it did lead her to wonder—as she often found herself doing—in this case, about their future as adults.

Mrs. Gradgrind prohibits wondering and scolds her children for their ingratitude—At that moment, their mother broke off the conversation, having overheard it as she opened the door unobserved. As she usually did, she shamed them for their behavior, making them responsible for her ill health and emphasizing their ingratitude toward their father for such an outstanding education, which they obviously did not appreciate. She blamed Tom for influencing Louisa, but Louisa denied it, saying that only the sparks from the fire had made her think of how short life was and how little promise her own life held. To her mother, this was nonsense, and she resorted to her usual tactic of prohibiting her children from speaking about such things. She then tried to make them feel guilty by wishing she had never had a family. As she sank into a chair, exhausted from her speech, she concluded illogically that then they would understand what it was like to be without her.

Chapter 9—Sissy's Progress

Sissy's difficulties in school—Sissy Jupe was having a hard time in school. In today's pop psychology terms, she would be considered more right-brained than left-brained, so all the calculating and analyzing she was required to do by Mr. M'Choakumchild did not sit well with her, nor did her answers to his questions please him. It was not just an issue of giving the wrong answer: in addition to not having a head for facts and figures, she habitually misunderstood the thrust of the question. When asked, for example, about the main principle of political economy, she responded with the Golden Rule ("Do unto others …"), which led both her teacher and Mr. Gradgrind to conclude that her training would be long and arduous and require a great deal of discipline.

Unhappiness at home—Her home life was no better. Although, by Louisa's estimate, she was kinder and more helpful to Mrs. Gradgrind than Louisa could ever be, Sissy only stayed because she believed that her father would return some day and would have wanted it so. Otherwise, there was a strong likelihood that she would have run away.

Sissy confesses her doubts to Louisa—In short, Sissy Jupe was not happy. One day, after Louisa tried to help her understand her academics a little better, Sissy blurted out how great it would be to be like her. Louisa was unconvinced, but the comment opened up an avenue for discussion that had remained closed until now. Blurting out her concerns, Sissy confessed to being terribly stupid, and Louisa's reassurance that things would improve seemed to make no impact. When Louisa asked her for details, Sissy, though ashamed at first, told her of several instances where she had clearly given Mr. M'Choakumchild the wrong answer. It was not that her answers didn't make sense from a human perspective, but they were not what he wanted to hear, and no other highly trained student would have even considered them.

Louisa asks about Sissy's background—When Sissy was done, it was clear that she felt utter shame from her failure, and, what's more, she didn't enjoy her schooling, even though it was what her father wanted. When she had recovered enough to look up at Louisa, Louisa asked her if her father was educated. Sissy hesitated at first, but when Louisa assured her that it was all right, she confessed that he was not. When Louisa asked about her mother, she discovered (again after some nervous hesitation) that she had been a dancer who died in childbirth, and according to her father, had been somewhat of a scholar. Louisa then asked whether her father had loved her mother, to which Sissy enthusiastically replied that he had loved her dearly and that his love for herself (meaning Sissy) had begun out of love for her mother. She added that she and her father had never been apart since she was a baby. That prompted Louisa to question that he had left her now, to which Sissy replied that it was only for her good and that he would never have done so otherwise and was sure to return.

More questions; Sissy's father's desire to educate her—Louisa then asked to know more about him, adding with sensitivity that she would not ask about it again. Where, for example, had they lived? Sissy explained that they had traveled constantly because of his work as a clown, again hesitating with a certain amount of dread before she said it. When Louisa asked whether he made people laugh, Sissy said yes but added that lately he had not been successful in doing so and had been coming home dejected. He felt afraid and inadequate in many ways, which was why he wanted her to be different from him by arming herself with an education. Louisa asked whether she had been his primary comfort, to which Sissy answered yes. He had loved to listen to her read, even though she had since learned that the books she read to him were "wrong." Listening to such tales as the Arabian Nights, however, took his mind off his troubles.

Only a single angry incident in a kind life—Louisa next wanted to know whether her father had always been kind. This drew an enthusiastic affirmative from Sissy, who said that he had only been angry once—with the dog Merrylegs, when the dog wouldn't cooperate with his request to perform a trick. It was after a failed performance, and her father had lost his temper and beaten the dog till it bled. Sissy had pleaded with her father to stop, which he finally did, and fortunately the dog forgave him, licking his face as he lay on the floor holding the dog in his arms and weeping.

Sissy witnesses her father's distress—By this time, Sissy herself was crying, so Louisa comforted her by taking her hand and giving her a kiss as she sat by her side. She then asked to hear the end of the story, assuring that she would take any blame it might incur. Sissy told her that she came home one day to find her father particularly distraught. He was trembling, crying, and holding himself as he kept repeating the words "My love!" and "My darling!"

Tom asks Louisa to visit with Bounderby; Sissy tells how her father abandoned her—At that moment, Tom entered, and though he showed no particular interest in their conversation, Louisa kindly asked him to give them a moment and not interrupt. He agreed but added that he wanted Louisa to come to the drawing room because Mr. Bounderby was there, and her presence would increase his chances of being asked to dinner by him. Promising to come soon, she continued her conversation with Sissy.

Sissy added that her father was convinced that he was a disgrace, having failed again to please his audience and that she would be better off without him. She tried to comfort him in whatever way she could, and after he had hugged and kissed her many times, he sent her on an errand to fetch the nine oils on the other side of town. When she asked whether she should take Merrylegs along, he said that she should take nothing of his. By the time she returned, he was gone.

Sissy's hope—Tom, who had decided to wait for "Loo," as he called her, interjected that she should do her best to look good for Mr. Bounderby. Sissy, who was now finished with her story, continued that she was convinced that her father would return some day, which was why she kept the nine oils for him. That was why, whenever the family received a letter, she a felt of pang of emotion and anticipation.

From then on, when Sissy would respectfully but repeatedly ask Mr. Gradgrind whether any mail had come for her, Louisa would watch with interest and sympathy as Sissy received the inevitable disappointing answer. Louisa was the only one with any empathy for the situation. Mr. Gradgrind lamented "Jupe's" lack of mental discipline and reason, which surely had not been the case had she been properly trained from a young age. Tom was becoming increasingly calculating as planned; and Mrs. Gradgrind could only think of her own discomfort at having to constantly listen to Sissy's requests. She would go on and on like this until Mr. Gradgrind's cold stare would finally silence her moaning.

Chapter 10—Stephen Blackpool

Coketown's inner city—Chapter 10 begins with a more detailed description of Coketown's inner city, a place where its hardworking citizens worked the hardest and where the town's already ugly cityscape was the ugliest. Dickens describes it as being a jumble of narrow streets and courts, all closely packed together so that the overall effect was one of claustrophobic disorder. The buildings were all brick and sported chimneys of multiple shapes, and the area was as polluted as it was devoid of nature. This area of brick buildings and narrow streets was one of the residential areas for the greater part of Coketown's population known as the "Hands," who were generally characterized by their hard lives; and among these Hands, there lived one Stephen Blackpool.

Stephen Blackpool—Stephen Blackpool was forty years old but looked older, the result of a particularly hard life. Dickens guessed that whatever good may originally have been his due went to someone else, and he in turn inherited that person's misfortunes. Commonly called "Old Stephen," he had long, thin gray hair, a stooped posture, and a serious expression. Unlike some Hands, he was neither talented, intelligent, nor accomplished; but he performed his power loom weaving job well, and he was a good man. Beyond that, there seemed to be nothing special about him.

Waiting for Rachael at the end of the workday—When we first meet Stephen, it is the end of the workday. The factory lights are all out, the machinery has stopped, and the Hands, which include men, women, and children, are now heading home. As he stood there watching the groups of women go by, shawls over their heads to ward off the rain, he was disappointed to discover that he had missed Rachael, a female factory worker he knew well. Finally, when they had all left, he headed home. Within three blocks, he suddenly recognized her and, calling her name, caught up and accompanied her the rest of the way.

Rachael—Rachael was thirty-five, also no longer young. Dickens describes her face as oval-shaped, dark, delicate, and quiet, with gentle eyes and black hair. Theirs was a respectful, affectionate relationship, being old, true friends. So when Stephen questioned her erratic timing going to and from work, she felt that they could be honest with each other, and she voiced her opinion that it might be better if they didn't walk together all the time. To never do so would be too hard for both of them, but being careful would help them avoid the gossip. Stephen admitted that her company meant a great deal to him—it was a precious bright spot in his life. At one point, she gently teased him about always being in a "muddle," as he called it, which elicited a good-natured response from him as he laughed at himself. When they arrived at her street, she placed her hand in his and bid him good night. As he watched her disappear down the dark street into one of the houses, it was clear that he loved her deeply.

Dickens's use of setting as a mirror of mood—As Stephen headed home, he occasionally looked up at the sky. The rain had stopped now, and the clouds were clearing, leaving a bright moon overhead. As he so often does, Dickens equates the surroundings with the characters' moods and thoughts, and in this case, the clearing sky seemed a direct reflection of Stephen's brighter mood. He turned down another narrow street and entered a building with a shop on the lower floor. Taking a candle, he lit it and proceeded up the stairs to his room.

Stephen's simple apartment—Dickens describes Stephen's room as being neat, clean, and adequately furnished. His remark that it had seen the "black ladder" several times was a reference to the black ladder kept by the undertaker for that area. It was the undertaker's practice to let the dead bodies of former tenants slide out the window of their apartments to their final destination. In other words, several of the previous tenants in Stephen's apartment had died, which had left its mark on the room's atmosphere.

Stephen's estranged drunken wife returns—As Stephen walked over to the fireplace to put down his candle, he nearly tripped over something on the floor. It turned out to be a filthy, disheveled, drunken woman, who now propped herself up on one arm. Recognizing her, he stepped back as he exclaimed, aghast with surprise, that she had returned. After cursing and mocking him in her hoarse voice, she stood up in her drunken manner, and leaning against the wall, threatened to return and sell him off as many times as she cared to. Then, claiming it as her right, she threw him off the bed, where he had been sitting in dismay with his hands covering his face. That night, Stephen slept in a chair while she snored the night away.

Chapter 11—No Way Out

Dickens's imaginative descriptions—Chapter 11 begins by describing the start of a new workday in Coketown. What is most intriguing here is not what Dickens describes but how he goes about it. His method is the opposite of the dull factual mentality that dominates Coketown and is the source of its misery. In fact, his description is entirely fanciful as it gathers the various imaginative analogies used so far into one place. The factories are "fairy palaces" bursting into light; the streams of smoke from the chimneys are "monstrous serpents; " and the factory machines are "melancholy mad elephants," ready to return to work.

God's works versus man's artifice—To Stephen, the noisy roomful of looms must not have seemed so imaginative. Yet, in Dickens's view, the quiet concentration of the faces of the loom workers had a dignity that only grew stronger when set against the noisy thrashing motions of the machinery. To him, it depicted the juxtaposition of God's Nature with man's artifice; and no matter how useful or efficient the latter might be, the former had an undeniable mystery that none of man's devices could approach.

Stephen visits Mr. Bounderby—At noon, when the bell rang, and the machines were all turned off for the lunch hour, Stephen exited the mill with the rest of the Hands. But except for a piece of bread, today he did not take lunch with the others. Instead, he walked to Mr. Bounderby's house on the hill, where he knocked on the door and requested permission to see Mr. Bounderby. Having always done his work steadily and never wished for anything more, Stephen passed the "acceptable employee" test and was admitted to the parlor, where Bounderby was dining on sherry and some kind of chop, and Mrs. Sparsit (who as a point of discipline never ate lunch) was doing needlework by the fire. Mr. Bounderby inquired as to his purpose, and when Stephen glanced over at Mrs. Sparsit, Bounderby immediately insisted that Mrs. Sparsit, being the highborn lady that she was, should be allowed to remain in her place. Blushing a bit, Stephen hoped that what he had to say would not offend her, and then, encouraged by Mr. Bounderby, proceeded to present his case.

Stephen seeks Bounderby's advice in relation to his marriage—Stephen's reason for being there was to seek advice from Mr. Bounderby. Nineteen years earlier, he had married a young, pretty girl who had since gone bad, even though he was a good husband. Mr. Bounderby interrupted to say that he was familiar with the tale, figuring that she had started drinking, quit her job, and, following that, made a general mess of things. Stephen continued that he had been extremely patient and tried twenty times to help her overcome her ways, but without success. He had suffered tremendously, staying out all night rather than going home, and he even considered throwing himself off the bridge but couldn't bring himself to do it. Finally, he arranged to pay her to stay away so that he could resume a life with some semblance of sanity. That worked for five years, until last night, when he found her lying on the floor by the fireplace.

Bounderby replied that, except for the last part, he had already been aware of this story. Relating it to her own misfortune, Mrs. Sparsit asked whether there had been a large age difference between Stephen and his wife. He answered that, no, they had been just a year or so apart. He then came to his main point: he wanted to know if there was a way that he could be rid of her, and he admitted that the only source of his sanity all these years had been another woman—the best woman alive, who had been a terrific comfort to him. Though somewhat shocked at the suggestion of getting rid of his wife, Mrs. Sparsit guessed correctly that if he could do so, he would marry the other woman. To this he agreed and then asked Mr. Bounderby whether there was a way to accomplish this.

Stephen inquires about the law—Unfortunately, the answer was no. First of all, he had married for better or worse, and the sanctity of marriage was to be upheld. Second, no matter how he tried to eliminate her from his life, there would be a law against it. It didn't matter if he hurt her, fled from her, or married someone else—there was a law against it. But Stephen Blackpool was not to be so easily deterred. His was an especially difficult case, and he had come to know what law there was to help him.

A disappointing answer—Finally, Bounderby admitted that there was, in fact, such a law, but to take advantage of it cost a great deal of money and was, therefore, not an option for common folk. It would involve three lawsuits, an Act of Parliament to permit the second marriage, and a cost of between a thousand to three thousand pounds. Dejected, Stephen concluded that it was all a muddle and that he would be better off dead. This prompted an indignant speech from Bounderby, who insisted that Stephen's sole duty was to attend to his piecework and not to judge the laws of the country. Furthermore, he reiterated that marriage was for better or worse, and there was, therefore, not much that could be done about it. Bounderby concluded that Stephen was making a mistake by expecting more out of life than was rightfully his to wish for.

On that note, Stephen thanked him somewhat dejectedly and left the two of them to their day—Mr. Bounderby to his self-admiration and Mrs. Sparsit to her needlework and her disappointment with the morals of the common folk.

Chapter 12—The Old Woman

Stephen meets an elderly lady outside Bounderby's house—As Stephen was crossing the street in this dejected state, his eyes fixed upon the ground, he felt someone touch his arm. Looking up in the highly focused manner of someone who worked around noise all day, Stephen saw a tall, elderly, well-proportioned woman, whose simple, clean clothing suggested a person from the countryside dressed up for a special occasion. Her shawl, umbrella, and muddy shoes further suggested that she had been traveling and had made a special trip to the city. Indicating Mr. Bounderby's house, she asked Stephen if he had just come from there, whether he had seen the owner, how he looked, and whether he was healthy. She seemed to already know a terrific deal about his appearance and manner, and as she spoke, Stephen thought he recognized her, though he couldn't be sure, and whatever memory he did have seemed unfavorable. When he confirmed all her questions, she thanked him with a great deal of satisfaction.

The elderly lady's annual trip to Coketown—As she continued walking with Stephen, he tried to be hospitable by making small talk with her. She informed him that she had come forty miles by third-class rail, that she had walked nine miles to reach the station, and that she was determined to do it again, if necessary. She seemed pleased with herself that she was capable of such stretches at her age. Stephen counseled her to not do it too often, to which she promptly agreed, claiming that it was strictly an annual event. Every year, she claimed, she would come to walk around the town and watch the gentlemen. This year she was disappointed that Mr. Bounderby had not yet shown himself, but she was prepared to make do with the fact that Stephen had seen him, and she had seen Stephen. This seemed strange to Stephen, who suddenly noticed the time on the church clock and sped up his pace. He was on his way back to work and needed to hurry. This did not bother the woman, who kept right up with him. "Was he happy?" she wanted to know. Not wanting to ruin her illusions about Coketown, he evaded the question by saying that everyone had his troubles. She guessed he must be referring to his home life, since she couldn't believe that a gentleman like Bounderby would allow trouble at work.

Pleasure in all things related to Coketown—As they approached the factory, the bell that called the workers back from lunch had already begun to ring, and the Hands were all filing back into the building. To the old woman, the sound was beautiful music, and as Stephen kindly shook her hand while saying goodbye, she asked him how long he had worked there and insisted on kissing his hand when she found out it had been twelve years. This seemed strange to him, but he couldn't help noticing that there was something natural and harmonious about her that he couldn't quite explain. Half an hour later, his meeting with the old woman was still running though his mind, when he happened to look out the window and see her still standing there, gazing admiringly at the factory. She did not seem bothered by the grime, the noise, and the smoke, which somehow transmuted itself in her mind into something glorious.

Stephen puts off going home—Eventually, she left, and when the bell finally rang, and the lights and machines in the factories were turned off for the day, Stephen's thoughts began to turn to that now dreaded place he called home. He did not go there directly, but ate first and then wandered about the town in the cold and wet. Tonight, Rachael's gentle, calming presence would have been a welcome relief, but she had gone home earlier, in keeping with her suggestion that they should avoid walking together quite so much. He and Rachael had known each other since they were young, and only the fact of his miserable marriage had prevented their own union. He thought with remorse about how she had sacrificed the joys of a family life for him, and he wondered how such a miserable, demonic wretch could dominate the fortunes of one so gracious and kind. Thinking on these things, he finally made his way home.

Chapter 13—Rachael

The inequality of life and death—As Stephen finally wandered home, he couldn't help thinking of the inequality of life and death. Somehow it didn't seem right to him that a miserable brute like the woman who now occupied his bed could continue living, while whole families mourned the loss of a beloved husband and father.

Stephen finds Rachael tending his wife—As he entered his room, he was surprised to find it calm and quiet. Rachael had been taking care of his wife and was sitting by the bed, which now had a curtain drawn across it. She had changed his wife's clothes and swept and tended the fire, and as he looked at her face, he could see through his own tears that she was crying.

She was glad to see him and commented on the late hour. He explained that he had been walking. When she mentioned that it was a rough night to be out in such weather, he agreed but realized that he hadn't noticed until now. Rachael said that she had been there earlier that day. The landlady called at around dinnertime to tell her that there was someone there who needed to be looked after—someone who was hurt and wandering about. She added that she came because she had known his wife long ago when they worked together because he had married her and because she believed that his merciful heart would not want the woman to suffer and die from lack of care. She mentioned the parable of the adulterous woman who was accused by the Pharisees, adding that she did not believe that he would be one to cast a stone at someone in such a miserable condition.

Rachael dresses his wife's wounds—Stephen, who now sat slumped in a chair, groaned as he listened to her. On hearing Rachael's last remark, he cried out her name. She responded by saying that he had suffered a great deal and that she was his humble, steadfast friend. Rachael then turned to the woman in the bed and dressed the wounds on her neck with bandages soaked in a basin containing liquid from one of two bottles that stood on a small three-legged table she had moved to the bedside. Looking closely at the bottle that she held in her hand, he blanched when he realized what the letters spelled out.

Rachael informed him that the procedure would need to be repeated at three in the morning, after which she would return home. He protested that she needed her sleep, but she replied that she would be all right and that he was more in need of sleep than she. As he listened to the wind and thunder outside, he marveled at how her gentleness had dispelled his anger, which now took the form of an external storm, kept at bay by her. She mentioned that his wife had not recognized her and did not seem lucid. According to the doctor, though, she was expected to be in a better frame of mind by the next day.

Feelings of fear and hope—Stephen shuddered when he looked at the bottle again, and when Rachael asked whether he had the chills, he explained that he was frightened. Suddenly, he stood up, shaking as he held the mantle to support himself. As she moved to help him, he motioned her to stop. He wanted her to stay by the bedside as he had seen her upon entering. He had been deeply moved by her mercy and goodness, and he wanted to preserve the image in his mind.

Once he stopped shaking, he sat down again, and looking at Rachael, it seemed to him in the glow of the candlelight, through his teary eyes that her head was surrounded by a halo. She quietly expressed her hope that his wife would leave again and stop troubling him once she improved. But now, she said, he should sleep.

Stephen's horrible dream—As his consciousness gradually faded, he began to dream. He saw himself at the altar, and though the woman was someone he cherished, he was surprised to note that she was not Rachael. As he looked around at the people, he recognized the faces of those both living and dead. Suddenly, darkness descended, followed by a great light that sprang from the illuminated words on a table of commandments upon the altar. These same letters seemed to light up the whole room and emit voices that filled the church. Then, all at once, the scene transformed. Stephen and the minister now stood outside in the daytime before a multitude of people, and it seemed to him that every one of them hated him, without a shred of mercy anywhere. He was standing on a platform beneath his loom. Dickens implies that the loom changed its shape into something else as Stephen looked at it. He then became aware that his own burial service was being read, and with that, the platform fell through and Stephen with it.

Somehow in his dream he was returned to his normal life, but he was now cursed: never, for the rest of eternity, would he ever be able to see or hear Rachael again. He was condemned to ceaselessly wander in search of something that forever eluded him. Worse, he was tormented by a horrible, terrifying shape that loomed before him in everything he saw. Everything he looked at seemed to change into that shape and the word that accompanied it and his whole life was taken up with trying to hide it from others; yet it pursued him wherever he went.

Stephen and his wife awaken—Gradually, Stephen became aware that he was back in his room, with the wind and the rain raging outside. The fire was spent, and Rachael was sleeping, kept warm by her shawl. As Stephen's eyes focused on the table by the bedside, he recognized the frightening shape from his nightmare standing upon it. He then noticed a movement in the curtain. Before long, he saw a hand and then the whole curtain pulled aside to reveal a wretched woman scanning the room with wild eyes. At first, they passed over the dark corner where he sat, but then came back. As she shaded her eyes with her hand to get a better look, it seemed to Stephen that she instinctively knew that he was there. Looking at her, he could not help thinking how there was not a shred remaining in that wild, depraved face of the young woman he had married so long ago.

Rachael awakens in time to save Stephen's wife from poisoning herself—Eventually, her gaze landed on the two bottles on the table, and after contemplating them a bit, she took a mug and uncorked the bottle containing the deadly poison, though she evidently didn't know this. The whole time she had been staring around the room, Stephen had been frozen, unable to speak or move. Nor was he certain that what he was viewing was real, thinking it might be a dream. But as she lifted the mug to her lips, he found his whole being silently screaming for Rachael to awaken. And she did—just in time to grab the mug from the hand of his wretched wife, even though it meant having her hair pulled and her forehead scratched.

Rachael dresses her wounds and prepares to leave—At that moment, the bell from the church clock struck three, and Stephen, now finally able to move, checked with Rachael to make sure he was not dreaming. Rachael now poured the dangerous liquid into the basin, where she soaked the linen to apply to the other woman, who now lay quietly in the bed. Afterwards, calm as ever, she disposed of the rest of the liquid and the bottle, which she broke. Having finished with everything, she wrapped herself in her shawl as she prepared to go out into the night.

Stephen blesses his angel—Stephen offered to walk her home, but she declined, saying it was only a minute away. When they arrived at the stairs outside the room, he asked her whether she wasn't afraid to leave him alone with the woman. Not sure what he meant, she uttered his name questioningly. In that moment, he knelt down before her, calling her an angel and blessing her. She protested that she was just his humble friend, a mere working woman with many weaknesses, but he insisted that she had changed his bad thoughts to good ones—that she had saved his soul. He continued, saying that he had come home in a desperate state and that when he had seen the bottle of poison, he couldn't be sure what he might do. Gasping, Rachael moved to cover her mouth with her hands, but Stephen took them in his, saying how her presence by the bedside had calmed him in his sleep, how he would never again think of his wife but always of her, and that he would steadfastly look forward to the day when they would be together in heaven. Both deeply emotional, they bid each other good night, and Rachael left.

The sky clears to reveal the stars—Outside, the wind still blew, but the rain had cleared, and the stars now shone brightly in the sky. Stephen stood in the street as he watched Rachael vanish in the darkness. To him, this gentle woman was like the stars shining down on his otherwise ordinary life.

Chapter 14—The Great Manufacturer

Time, the great producer of change—Dickens begins Chapter 14 with a fanciful description of time, calling it the "great manufacturer" and likening it to a large piece of machinery that churns perpetually onward. But unlike the humdrum sameness of Coketown, time produced change.

Tom and Louisa grow into young adulthood; Tom becomes Bounderby's apprentice—As time passed, Mr. Gradgrind noticed how both Louisa and Thomas were maturing and on the verge of adulthood. Louisa was turning into a young woman, and Thomas had grown an entire foot. Contemplating his son, Mr. Gradgrind concluded that it was time to apprentice him to Mr. Bounderby, so off Tom went to work in Bounderby's bank and live in his home.

Sissy Jupe grows into a lovely young woman; Mr. Gradgrind gives up on her education—Time had also "manufactured" Sissy Jupe into a lovely young woman, though no more intelligent than before, despite all the effort expended on her education. Mr. Gradgrind and Sissy were both agreed on this subject, just as they were agreed that she had tried hard. Still, Mr. Gradgrind was deeply disappointed by her inadequate progress and concluded that there was no point in continuing—that they had begun too late and that her early childhood circumstances had perhaps been unsuitable preparation.

A place for Sissy Jupe—Apologetic yet grateful for all Mr. Gradgrind had done for her, Sissy wished that she could have done better. But Mr. Gradgrind was both reasonable and pragmatic. He would not have her shedding tears, and he was as capable of acknowledging her good points as her bad ones. Despite her intellectual failings, he could see that she was a good person, useful around the home, affectionate and serious. There was also something indefinable about her, something that defied calculation yet won him over nonetheless.

Mr. Gradgrind makes an appointment with Louisa—Time had also wrought a change in Mr. Gradgrind, who was now a member of Parliament, in charge of weights and measures. But to return to Louisa … One day, Mr. Gradgrind noticed that she had quietly gone from being almost a young woman to having actually become one. Several nights later, as he was leaving for the evening and bidding her goodbye, he asked her to come speak to him in the morning, indicating that they had something important to discuss.

Tom hints to Louisa of something in the works—Later that same evening, as Louisa was watching the fire, her brother Tom happened to come by for a quick visit. He hinted to her about what was going on between Bounderby and their father, who were having a serious conference at the bank that evening. He further suggested that the reason they had chosen the bank was to keep the conversation as far out of Mrs. Sparsit's earshot as possible. Finally, he hinted that if she decided to do whatever it was he knew about (though he didn't say more), they could both be together much more often—which would do them both good.

Louisa wonders about her future—At no point did she hint that she had any idea what he meant, and the chapter ends as she watches him disappear into the distance to join some friends. As she stands there looking out over the city of Coketown, there is a sense of uncertainty, a wondering about what Time—that ancient great manufacturer—would weave next in the life of this young woman.

Chapter 15—Father and Daughter

Mr. Gradgrind's blue study, the seat of his calculated decision-making activities—The many blue books that lined the walls of Mr. Gradgrind's study gave the room an overall blue appearance, prompting Dickens to momentarily compare him to Bluebeard, the mythical tyrant who murdered all his wives. Although he notes that Gradgrind was nothing like Bluebeard, it was here in this blue room—like an astronomer in an observatory without windows—that he would decide the fates, through pure calculation, of the masses of people he had never seen. And it was here, too, that he had calculated his own daughter's fate.

No interfering emotions—To Gradgrind, of course, that sort of calculation was a good thing. So when Louisa appeared in the morning to discuss the earnest subject mentioned by her father on the previous evening, there were few, if any, wayward emotions to interfere with the factual approach he would recommend, and whatever few there were on either side were quickly squashed out of existence or brushed over as though they had never existed to begin with.

Mr. Gradgrind presents Bounderby's marriage proposal—His first step, therefore, in approaching her was to remind her of her excellent training and his confidence that she would see its merit in considering the proposal he was about to present. To this she said nothing. After waiting a moment, he explained that he had received a request for her hand in marriage. Once more, she was silent. When he repeated the statement, she assured him she was listening. Pleased with her utter lack of emotion, which he deemed evidence of the success of her education, he took a moment to gather his thoughts and then presented her with the facts: Mr. Bounderby has asked her to consider his marriage proposal.

Louisa and her father discuss the proposal; Mr. Gradgrind avoids the word "love"—After a heavy silence, Louisa finally asked her father whether he thought she loved Mr. Bounderby. Somewhat disturbed by this question, Mr. Gradgrind replied that he could not answer that question, so Louisa rephrased it: Was she expected to love Mr. Bounderby? Her father answered that he did not ask her to do so, so she pressed further along the same lines: Did Mr. Bounderby want her to love him? Again, her father tried to skirt the issue, but she was adamant, so he resorted to reason and calculation to sort out the matter. First of all, it depended on what was meant by "love," and Mr. Bounderby was certainly not so irrational as to expect any whimsical emotions to interfere with good judgment. When Louisa asked which term she should use in its place, Mr. Gradgrind once more stressed the importance of fact versus emotion, which was for the foolish masses. The only potential issue he could see with the marriage proposal was the thirty-year discrepancy in their ages, Louisa being twenty and Bounderby fifty. Yet it was a fact not only in England but in many other countries that such an age discrepancy was a standard thing and, therefore, not to be considered a drawback. Other than that, judging purely according to their respective life stations and resources, they were equals. Still not satisfied, Louisa repeated her previous question: What term should she use in place of the one she had previously suggested (namely, "love," though Gradgrind was careful to never utter the actual word)? Again, he skirted the issue, treating it as an irrelevancy. The sole question with which she should concern herself was: "Shall I marry him?"

Louisa ponders the question "Shall I marry him?"—She slowly repeated the words. To her father's satisfaction, she acknowledged that she did not harbor the poor habits of thought so common to other young women. Having thoroughly stated his case, her father now left her to make her own decision. As they sat there regarding each other, there was an instant when her father might have noticed how Louisa wanted to open herself to him and, in a fit of affection and trust, reveal her true feelings. But the moment was too short, and the walls he had built through years of reason and calculation were too high. And so, the moment was lost to both of them.

Louisa's imaginative spirit asserts itself for a moment—Louisa turned her gaze to the distant smokestacks of Coketown for a long time, which finally prompted her father to ask whether she was consulting them. She replied that though they had a dreary sameness about them during the daytime, at night, they would burst forth with fire. For the first time during the conversation, she seemed excited. Her father, however, could not see the point of the statement.

Louisa accepts halfheartedly—Changing the subject slightly, she said that since life was so short, she wished to make the most of it to the small extent that she could. But then she waved the statement aside with the conclusion, "What does it matter?" Somewhat confused, Gradgrind asked what she meant by her last sentence. She returned the conversation to the previous question: "Shall I marry him?" Her answer, which she wanted her father to repeat word for word to Mr. Bounderby was that since Bounderby wanted to take her that she would accept his offer. All this was said unemotionally and deliberately, which pleased her father. When he asked whether she had any preferences as to the timing of the wedding, she replied that she did not, again saying, "What does it matter?" This prompted him to ask her whether anyone else had proposed to her. This question seemed ridiculous to her since she had spent her entire life sheltered from people, emotions, and life experiences—namely, from the factors needed to create that possibility. Furthermore, the part of her nature that might have harbored any preferences or imaginings had been thoroughly squashed by facts and calculations since she was a small child. In fact, she felt, she had never truly been a child—never thought or felt or dreamt like one. This, along with her sober decision to marry Bounderby, once again pleased her father, who counted his daughter's practical wisdom a proof of educational success.

Gradgrind informs his wife of the marriage—All that remained now was to inform her mother, so after kissing Louisa and congratulating her on her choice, they proceeded to the drawing room, where he presented his daughter as Mrs. Bounderby. Mrs. Gradgrind, who apparently had known about the proposal, congratulated Louisa, but not without first inquiring whether her health was good enough to sustain the burden of marriage. Having made a similar decision years ago, she noted that she started having splitting headaches soon after becoming a wife. Nevertheless, the situation called for congratulations—but goodness me! now Mrs. Gradgrind had to decide what to call her new son-in-law, since neither Mister, Josiah, nor Joe would do. With no help from the rest of them in deciding this momentous question, Mrs. Gradgrind slipped back into her usual lifeless condition after voicing her request that the wedding take place as soon as possible so that she wouldn't have to hear about the topic anymore.

Louisa's attitude toward Sissy turns cold—Sissy, who had witnessed the entire scene, was overwhelmed with a variety of feelings on hearing the news—from sympathy and sadness to astonishment and misgiving. None of this escaped Louisa, and from then on their relationship changed as Louisa became cold and distant.

Chapter 16—Husband and Wife

Mr. Bounderby tells Mrs. Sparsit of his upcoming wedding—On discovering that his proposal had been accepted, Mr. Bounderby realized that one of his first obligations would be to tell Mrs. Sparsit and this made him uncomfortable. He could not predict how she would react and, therefore, did not know how to approach the matter. Finally, he decided to buy some smelling salts in case she fainted at the announcement.

For all his thought and effort at mitigating the situation, Mr. Bounderby approached Mrs. Sparsit with an air of guilt and shame. She was doing her usual needlework by the fireplace, and after they cordially greeted each other, he seated himself and prepared to deliver the news. For a while, they sat silently as she continued with her work. Finally, she looked up at him. After complimenting her on her noble breeding and excellent sense, he warned her that he was about to give her a shock. Mrs. Sparsit calmly set down her clothwork and regarded Mr. Bounderby attentively. With that, Bounderby informed her of his impending marriage to Louisa Gradgrind.

Mrs. Sparsit calmly congratulates Mr. Bounderby; Mrs. Sparsit prepares to move—Contrary to Bounderby's expectations, Mrs. Sparsit neither fainted nor threw a fit. Instead, she congratulated him, and with a superior yet sympathetic air, she gave him her sincere wishes for his happiness. This bothered Bounderby, who had anticipated a completely different reaction and now found himself resenting her response. Nevertheless, he thanked her in an equally cordial manner and welcomed her to stay, if she chose to do so. If not, there was a similar position at the bank for a lady of her social standing. She would have all the amenities—her own living quarters, an annual stipend, candles, coal, and all the other comforts. Mrs. Sparsit declined the first offer, evidently considering the idea of living with him and his new wife improper. However, she gratefully accepted the offer for the position at the bank as long as it didn't diminish her social position. She completed her statements by again hoping that the new Mrs. Bounderby would turn out to be all he had hoped for.

The wedding date is set, and the wooing takes place—The wedding was scheduled to take place in eight weeks. Meanwhile, Mr. Bounderby wooed Louisa at Stone Lodge on a nightly basis, bringing her bracelets and having all sorts of things made for her—dresses, jewelry, gloves, cakes. Various agreements were also reached, presumably between Mr. Bounderby and Mr. Gradgrind, and as

Dickens says, all arrangements pertaining to the courtship were based on facts.

The wedding day, with a factual wedding breakfast—Eventually, the day of the wedding arrived, and Louisa and Bounderby were married in one of Coketown's churches, afterwards returning to Stone Lodge for breakfast. That occasion, too, which normally would have been joyful and celebratory, had a factual, no-nonsense tone. Every fact about the breakfast food and where it came from was known, and even the youngest bridesmaid displayed a practical intellectual savvy.

Following breakfast, Bounderby delivered a speech to his guests, thanking them for their good wishes and wishing them the same good fortune in finding a suitable wife or husband. As usual, he felt compelled to insert something about his background—how little he thought, all those years ago when he was a mere street urchin that we would ever marry Mr. Gradgrind's daughter. But now that he was a man of independent means and she a well brought-up young lady, he felt that they were worthy of each other.

Louisa's distress shows through on the way to the honeymoon—A short while later, as the couple prepared to leave for their honeymoon to Lyons, France (where Mr. Bounderby also had a factory and would be mixing pleasure with work), Louisa met her brother, Tom, on her way down the stairs. He was thrilled that she had been such a good sport and sister by marrying Bounderby, and he said as much. She did not share his feelings. As she hugged him tightly, it seemed that the cool, calm exterior she had worked so hard to preserve had begun to break down.

BOOK II: REAPING

Chapter 1—Effects in the Bank

Coketown: a city lost in pollution—Coketown was like any other extremely polluted city in the sense that, even on a sunny summer's day, it was impossible to distinguish the actual town from the smoke and filth rising from its chimneys. From a distance, it registered as a dense haze—and that was all. You could see nothing else.

Hypersensitivity of Coketown's leading businessmen—But exist it did, and it did that despite the millers' protests that every time they were called to task on some legal or humanitarian issue, they and their businesses were "ruined." It was not hard to make them feel that way, since they were hypersensitive to anything that would interfere with their efficiency or profitability. They even threatened to throw their businesses into the Atlantic Ocean if the government forced them to take responsibility for their deeds. Of course, as Dickens points out, they hadn't done this, thus ensuring not only Coketown's stability but its growth, as well.

The "eye of Heaven" turned evil through human carelessness—That particular summer's day was hot and bright enough that the sun was able to make its presence felt through the thick haze. The entire town smelled like oil, and the monotonous up-and-down movements and constant humming and whirring of the machines continued for as long as they remained on. Although the sun might have been a blessing in a more natural setting, here in Coketown—certainly in its industrial sections—this natural blessing became a deadly curse as it relentlessly baked the bricks and intensified the obnoxious, dire effects of the pollution. In one of Dickens's most important lines in the book, he says that even the "eye of Heaven" will turn into an "evil eye" when interfered with by human stupidity or immorality.

Mrs. Sparsit at the bank—The scene shifts to the bank and Mrs. Sparsit, who is sheltered by the shade of the manager's boardroom, where she spends her afternoons. When Mr. Bounderby arrives in the morning, she greets him from the third level, where she keeps her private quarters. The bank looks exactly like Mr. Bounderby's house, except that it is larger. On the whole, though, it blends perfectly with Coketown, and Mrs. Sparsit has become a familiar sight, sitting in the window with her needlework. While she views herself as the Bank Fairy, the townspeople see her as the Bank Dragon guarding the treasure.

Mrs. Sparsit's fellow bank employees—Mrs. Sparsit was not alone in the bank. She had the company of a light porter (the now grown Bitzer, who first defined a horse for Sissy Jupe) and a deaf servingwoman, who was supposed to be rich and due to be murdered. Mrs. Sparsit was in charge of the bank furniture and the vaults. At night, Bitzer would sleep by the vault on a trundle bed.

Mrs. Sparsit and Bitzer chat at teatime—In the afternoons, Bitzer would bring Mrs. Sparsit her tea, and they would chat. This afternoon was no different from the rest, so after he placed her tea on the leather boardroom table and knuckled his forehead out of respect, she began to ask him about the day's events. There was nothing new: the Hands were organizing themselves against the management, and except for onc indolent employee, all was otherwise well at the bank. Bitzer made the mistake at one point of mentioning the employee's name, but this was quickly corrected by Mrs. Sparsit, who had her reputation to uphold.

Bitzer's low opinion of the Hands—From there, the conversation led to the question of why most Coketowners (the Hands) could not follow the example of those who had made their fortunes from nothing. The theory was that if one person could do it, everyone could—a theory Bitzer now espoused along with his disdain for the Hands' amusements. He, after all, never needed amusement, being so perfectly trained in the regulated manner of Coketown's governors.

A gentleman stranger knocks at the door—As Mrs. Sparsit and Bitzer were conversing, Bitzer noticed a man knocking at the bank's outside door. It turned out that the stranger, a well-bred, rather lackadaisical gentleman, had arrived by train not long ago and was looking for Mr. Bounderby's house. He had a letter to deliver and had been misdirected to the bank. However, on seeing Mrs. Sparsit in the window, he thought she might know where to find Mr. Bounderby. It seemed, though, that the visitor was not exclusively interested in Mr. Bounderby. In fact, he seemed more interested in Mrs. Bounderby, who was reputed to be cold, hardhearted, and brilliant, an impression he had received from her father, whom he knew through his brother's membership in the House of Commons. After asking a number of questions about her, he finally went on his way.

Chapter 2—Mr. James Harthouse

Mr. James Harthouse—Mr. James ("Jem") Harthouse initially came to Coketown because of Mr. Gradgrind's recruiting efforts, having tried a number of other adventurous outlets for his time and energy, and finding none of them satisfactory. He had ridden with the cavalry, followed an English minister overseas, visited Jerusalem, and traveled around the world in a yacht. Sadly, it all bored him. Luckily, just at that time, Mr. Gradgrind's group happened to be looking for new members. And so, Mr. Harthouse now found himself amidst the proverbial grime and smoke of Coketown, complete with a letter of introduction to Mr. Bounderby from Mr. Gradgrind himself. Harthouse had been referred to Gradgrind's group by his brother, a well-known and particularly witty member of the House of Commons, who had gotten the general attention by putting a widow's cap on a dead cow that was killed in a train wreck.

Bounderby meets Harthouse—Mr. Bounderby picked Mr. Harthouse up from the hotel in Coketown. As usual, he was full of blustering and boasting—the tales of his destitute childhood, the lordly but futile aspirations of Coketown's Hands, and his own utter lack of breeding. Mr. Harthouse listened to all this in as gentlemanly a manner as he could.

Harthouse's fascination with Louisa—One thing, however, had gained Mr. Harthouse's otherwise jaded attention and that was the description of Louisa Gradgrind Bounderby. The reality did not disappoint. Though young and attractive, she was much more than that. Unlike most girls her age, she had a complexity about her that was difficult to decipher, and she never seemed to be fully at ease. In fact, until her brother entered the room later in the evening, she never even smiled but guarded every thought, movement, and word with an unusual degree of watchfulness and discipline. Even the house itself and its furnishings displayed no comforting feminine touch, instead exhibiting only Mr. Bounderby's heavy hand.

Harthouse's lackadaisical attitude surprises Louisa—On asking Harthouse about his opinions and intentions in taking his current post, Louisa discovered to her surprise that he had none—at least, none that were backed by enough strength of character to merit the name of "opinion." To him, one opinion was as good as another, and most, if not all, were worthless. He had, therefore, decided to follow her father's lead, especially since he espoused facts and figures.

Bounderby introduces Harthouse to Coketown's leading citizens—Before dinner, Mr. Bounderby took Mr. Harthouse to visit the more notable figures living in and around Coketown. Mr. Harthouse had coached himself on facts and figures using several bluebooks, so he managed to present a convincing picture. Afterwards, they went to dinner, where Mr. Bounderby, as always, entertained them with stories of some of the more disgusting meals he had had as a child. Louisa maintained her usual stern look, while Harthouse feigned appropriate gentlemanly enthusiasm.

Harthouse meets Tom and sees Louisa smile for the first time—Though there were only three at dinner, Mr. Harthouse noticed that the table was set for four. So far, the identity of the fourth person remained unknown. But then the door opened, and as young Thomas Gradgrind entered, Louisa's face broke into a lovely smile for the first time. Dickens refers to young Tom as "the whelp" and notes that he was not half as gracious to his sister, or anyone else, for that matter. He especially disliked Bounderby and made no attempt to hide his feelings. To Harthouse's question as to whether he recognized him from public school (which is private school in England) or overseas, the answer was "No"—Tom had been educated at home. Harthouse, though not obvious about it, took a liking to Tom; and when Harthouse needed an escort back to the hotel later that evening, Tom was eager to offer him company.

Chapter 3—The Whelp

Young Tom's waywardness—For all the Gradgrind rules and regulations, facts and figures, young Thomas Gradgrind still did not exhibit the straightforward discipline and discretion that had in part been the object of his training. Nor did he have any great degree of insight or foresight. It came, therefore, as no surprise when, on arriving at the hotel, he gladly accepted Mr. Harthouse's invitation to accompany him upstairs for a drink and a cigar.

Harthouse observes Tom's lack of discretion—Tom admired Mr. Harthouse. He had an ease and elegance about him that was seldom, if ever, seen in a town like Coketown. Tom's admiration did not escape Mr. Harthouse, who was more used to exercising all the qualities that Tom lacked. It seemed strange to him that Tom was so quick to express his sarcastic feelings about "old Bounderby," as Tom liked to call him. Whether they were true was less influential than voicing them in a discreet manner, but this was not something that Tom was prone to do.

Tom's view that Louisa married Bounderby for him—The conversation then turned to Louisa's attitude toward her husband, and Tom was quick to offer that she liked him no better than he did. She had the advantage of being a girl, though, and girls could adjust more easily to various situations—or so he thought. Besides, "Loo" had never had a lover before, so when "old Bounderby" made the proposal through their father, there was nothing to stop her from saying yes. Add to that her brother's pressure to marry Bounderby in order to satisfy his own needs (after all, what needs did she have?), and was it any wonder that she was so dutiful?

Girls have fewer needs—Of course, Tom didn't view himself as selfish. He was quite satisfied that he had had such an easy time persuading his sister to sacrifice her own life for his sake by taking on the role of Josiah Bounderby's wife. But he didn't see it that way. He was convinced that girls that fewer needs and more mental and emotional resources to keep themselves entertained and contented under the worst of conditions. He knew that Louisa didn't feel that way about herself, but he was still convinced that she wouldn't mind.

Tom falls asleep on the couch—Mr. Harthouse mentioned that he had seen Mrs. Sparsit at the bank the previous day and that she, too, seemed to hold Louisa in admiration. Tom corrected him. It was more than that: indeed, Mrs. Sparsit was affectionately devoted to his sister. Having uttered these words,

Tom, who by now had had several drinks, promptly fell asleep on the couch, where he had been lying for almost the entire time.

Dickens's dark spin on Tom's lack of discretion—He awoke to the news that it was late and that he should be leaving. Not yet entirely awake, he made his way to the street, where he finally found his way home and to his bed. Still referring to him as a "whelp," Dickens ends the chapter with the ominous remark that if he had been a better brother instead of such a whelp, he might instead of gone to the polluted river and drowned himself for what he had just done.

Chapter 4—Men and Brothers

Slackbridge moves to ostracize Stephen for not joining the union's cause—Chapter 4, "Men and Brothers," begins with a rabble-rousing speech appealing to the good people of Coketown to join together in rising up against the oppressive management that has misused them and their families for so long. The speaker, a man named Slackbridge, is greeted by enthusiastic cheers from a packed hall of faces, all more honest, more hardworking, and more manly than he. In fact, he was not there today to gain their support for a union cause but to turn them against one man who, for his own private reasons, would not join. That man turned out to be Stephen Blackpool, who was now brought to the stage, while the chairman had Slackbridge take his seat.

Old Stephen's defense: private reasons for refusing to join the union cause—In his thick northern English accent, Old Stephen tried to explain that his reasons for not joining reached far past the work situation at Bounderby's mill and that they were not likely to change. Slackbridge, who had been watching with a sarcastic look from his seat, leapt up when he heard that and tried to condemn Stephen as bringing destruction on all of them. Although there was some cheering, most of the listeners were quiet. Their sense of honor and fairness was too strong to condemn a man without a hearing, and they could see from Stephen's face the toll that his life had taken on him.

Stephen pointed out that Slackbridge was a paid speaker and that he should continue with his eloquence. It was not his duty to comprehend the burdens he had born—he alone could do that. Seeing Old Stephen's dignity, the hall fell silent, and the chairman called out to Slackbridge to hold his peace and let the man speak; and so, Stephen resumed.

Stephen asks for tolerance and understanding as he finishes his final shifts—Without mentioning details, Stephen once more explained that he had thought carefully about the situation and simply could not join the group. He knew that they would be bound by their sense of right to shun him for this, even if he lay bleeding in the street. He had concluded that there was no other way for him, and he felt no anger toward any of them for any reason, and never had throughout his lifetime. The chairman warned him to think carefully before making such a drastic decision, but Old Stephen was determined, and after holding his hands in the air in a gesture of reverence toward his fellow workers, he moved to leave but then remembered something else. He guessed that once the matter was settled, he would not be allowed in to work. Until then, his sole request was to let him in to do what he had done all his life so that he could earn his livelihood. Having delivered his final statement, he silently made his way through the audience and out the door.

Slackbridge reverts to rabble-rousing—Once Stephen had left, Slackbridge used his speaking talent to enliven the mood, which had grown somewhat quiet and doubting, since the men now had to contend with their consciences. Before long, though, the men were all cheering. The individual had to make way for the mass of workers in this case—their acts were justified.

Stephen's loneliness on being ostracized—And so, Stephen walked his lonely way, made lonelier by having once known some bit of recognition that now had turned into none at all. Even some of the women no longer behaved in the same way toward him, and he had not seen Rachael since the assembly four days earlier. Worse, he was especially afraid that Rachael would suffer because of his punishment.

Bitzer summons Stephen to Bounderby's home—That night, as he exited the factory, he was approached by Bitzer, the pale young man from the bank, who informed him that Mr. Bounderby wanted to see him. Flushed at first that anyone at all had spoken to him, Stephen turned around and made his way to the home of Mr. Bounderby.

Chapter 5—Men and Masters

Bounderby questions Stephen about his knowledge of union matters—So Stephen fulfilled his duty and went to Mr. Bounderby's house, and Mr. Bounderby, whom Dickens likens to a wind because of his blustering approach, questioned him about what he knew. Stephen, however, knew nothing, being innocent of the accusation that had been made against him. This did not satisfy Mr. Bounderby, who persisted with the line of questioning. When nothing was forthcoming, he began to make an example of Stephen to Mr. Harthouse, who had been conversing with Louisa on the couch.

Bounderby unfairly accuses Stephen—However, Bounderby's assessment was utterly wrong. Stephen was clear that he had nothing to say because he knew nothing, but Bounderby interpreted this as meaning that he was loyal to the last to his fellow workers, who had turned against him. Even when Stephen protested Bounderby's interpretation, Bounderby, in his usual blustering manner, insisted that he come out with the information. All Stephen would tell him was that he was sorry when the people had poor leaders. Bounderby asked him directly why he had not joined forces with the others, to which Stephen replied that he had made a promise to someone. Bounderby then pointedly asked whether Stephen would have joined if the issues revolving the management (himself) had been the only ones in question. To this Stephen answered in the affirmative. Pointing angrily at Stephen and equating him with "rascals and rebels," Bounderby asked Mr. Harthouse whether he had ever seen such a man in all his travels.

Stephen defends his fellow workers despite their betrayal of him—At this point, Stephen intuitively sought refuge in Louisa's face, and addressing her as "ma'am," he protested that his people were neither rebels nor rascals. He admitted that they had not been kind to him recently, but he was firmly convinced that they believed they were doing their duty. In his quiet, respectful way, he described them as affectionate, faithful, tender, and compassionate, and that they would rather be hurt themselves than ever change their nature. How it was that their good points regularly led them into trouble he did not understand, but it was indeed so. Yet his people were a patient lot and wanted to do right, and he could not believe that they were the entire cause of the problem.

Bounderby tries to entrap Stephen with Harthouse as a witness—Mr. Bounderby, who was bothered by the fact the Stephen had directed his attention toward someone other than himself, asked him whether he was sure that he had nothing more to tell them. When Stephen replied that he did not, Bounderby called Mr. Harthouse to witness a conversation between him and Stephen, since he wanted him to hear it firsthand rather than through hearsay. When Stephen seemed troubled by Harthouse's presence and turned again to Louisa for refuge, she quickly directed him with her eyes to face Mr. Bounderby instead. Mr. Bounderby then asked him point blank what it was he had come to complain about. Stephen replied that he had not come to complain but because he had been sent for. Intent on a particular response, Bounderby asked what his people generally complained about.

Prompted by Bounderby, Stephen speaks up for the poor—After a moment of hesitation, Stephen replied that he had never been one to express his observations but that he had certainly felt their weight. Look around, he said, pointing out the disparity between the rich and the poor in a town that was obviously wealthy. Look at the large numbers of the poor and the sameness of their lives—how they worked from cradle to grave without much in between to give their lives joy or meaning. And look at how they were spoken of and treated and written about, and how they were never in the right and always in the wrong. How could this not be a muddle? said Stephen, using one of his favorite expressions.

And how would you fix this "muddle?" asked Bounderby. Stephen protested that it was not for him to know that but for those in positions of authority. Furious by then, Bounderby announced that the solution was to send the dissenters to penal colonies. To Stephen, however, this was no solution. The problem had not begun with those who protested it, and it would not end by trying to physically eliminate them. The answer did not lie in force or in an unnatural division of right and wrong. Nor did the solution lie in just leaving things as they were. As long as people were treated like machines and not like human beings, with feelings, memories, likes and dislikes—in short, as if they had no souls—so long would things be not right, for it was nothing less than the unmaking of God's own work.

An infuriated Bounderby unjustly judges and terminates Stephen—By now, having been motioned to the door by Louisa's warning expression, Stephen stood there waiting to know whether Bounderby expected anything else of him. Completely forgetting why Stephen had come to begin with, a now red-faced Bounderby told him to stop. It seemed to him that Stephen was one of those fellows who always had something to complain about—that was now clear to him—and had he not informed him last time that complaints were not welcome and that if he had a grievance, he should turn around and leave? He added that Stephen was obviously so ill-natured that his own kind had rejected him. He could,

therefore, finish up whatever he was doing and leave town. Stephen replied that Bounderby must know

that if he couldn't find work with him, he was not likely to find it elsewhere. But Bounderby was cold and

adamant. As a last resort, Stephen looked once more toward Louisa, but by now she had averted her

eyes. As he exited the house, he sighed, and in his thick northern English accent, he quietly breathed:

"Heaven help us!"

Chapter 6—Fading Away

Stephen meets Rachael and the old woman—As Stephen made his way out of Bounderby's house and down the street, whom should he meet but the old woman accompanied by Rachael. It was late already, and night was falling fast, so Stephen fell in with the two women, walking between them to accompany them to their respective places. The old woman had arrived in town later in the year than usual, having been plagued with breathing problems and, therefore, decided to wait for warmer weather. She was especially excited to have read that Mr. Bounderby had been married, and she was determined to catch a glimpse of his wife, though she hadn't succeeded so far. In the process, she met Rachael, who seemed friendly enough to approach.

Stephen describes Louisa for the old lady; he explains that he will be leaving, and why—Again, Stephen felt an instinctive dislike for the old woman, but again, he could find no solid reason for doing so. Her qualities seemed as decent as the next person's, so he resolved to treat her with the same courtesy and kindness as he would yield to anyone else. His first move, therefore, was to describe Louisa to her, since that seemed to be her main interest at the moment. He described her as young, attractive, with a still manner and dark, "thinking" eyes. The old woman was ecstatic to hear such a good report, exclaiming that she must be a happy wife. Stephen said that he didn't know whether he could vouch for her happiness, to which the old woman replied that she must be happy if she was his master's wife. This led to the next subject—that Stephen and Bounderby had parted ways, and that Stephen would soon be leaving town. He still didn't know where he would go or what he would do, but he had determined that it was all for the best, both for Rachael and for him, even though it would be difficult for him to leave her. He felt lighter, he told her, and Rachael, unwilling to add to his hardship, comforted him with her smile.

Stephen invites the old woman and Rachael for tea—The old woman showed such an eagerness to ingratiate herself despite her increased physical challenges, that both Stephen and Rachael felt compassion for her, and Stephen was moved to invite them both for tea. So up to his small apartment they went, where he served them tea and lump sugar and fresh bread and butter—proof that the Coketown magnates were right in judging the Hands to be an extravagant, unthinking lot, especially since this little social get-together was entirely unplanned.

Stephen asks about the elderly lady, Mrs. Pegler, and her past—It occurred to Stephen as they sat enjoying their meal together that he had not yet asked the elderly lady her name. Mrs. Pegler, came the reply. Widowed? Oh, yes, for a long time now. Children? This elicited a nervous response from Mrs. Pegler as Rachael hinted that they were dead. Stephen apologized for bringing up a difficult subject, but Mrs. Pegler, her cup nervously clattering, explained that her one son had done exceedingly well but was not to be discussed, if that was all right. She explained that he was lost to her, and though it seemed that he was dead, there was something unusual in her manner.

Stephen learns that Louisa has arrived downstairs; Mrs. Pegler asks to hide in a corner—As Stephen was still apologizing for his blunder, his landlady entered and whispered something to him. On hearing the word "Bounderby," Mrs. Pegler leapt up and begged her host to hide her or at least to let her fade into a dark corner. Stephen explained that it was not Mr. Bounderby who had arrived but his wife. Still trembling, she asked to be ignored as much as possible as she took her place in the corner.

Louisa's first encounter with individual Hands—Louisa then entered with her brother Tom (the "whelp") in tow. Stephen and Rachael had both stood in the meantime and now waited for Louisa to address them. This was Louisa's first visit ever to the home of one of the Hands. Never before in her entire life had she been confronted with a Hand on an individual level. Until now, they had been presented to her as statistics, things to be calculated and maximized rather than people with lives and feelings. Sometimes they caused problems; sometimes they reaped rewards, but always, until now, they had been conceived of as a group, an idea, instead of the human beings that they were.

Louisa explains her desire to help and asks some questions—Finally, she broke the silence, explaining that she had come to hopefully be of service in the wake of this afternoon's conversation. She then asked Stephen if Rachael were his wife. Rachael's silent response suggested that she was not, and Louisa, blushing with embarrassment, apologized for her mistake, mentioning that she had not intended to cause pain and that if she should ask any other awkward questions, it was because she did not know how to speak to them. She then asked Rachael if she knew about what had transpired at Bounderby's that afternoon. Rachael replied that she had heard the outcome. In an effort to straighten out the facts, Louisa asked Rachael whether it was true that Stephen was unlikely to find work once he had been let go by one employer. Rachael confirmed the statement, saying that it was unlikely once he had gotten a bad name. How, Louisa wanted to know, was the term "bad name" defined? It meant that the person was a troublemaker. So if, Louisa continued, the person suffered from the prejudices of both the working and the ruling classes, that person stood no chance of finding work or acceptance between the two of them. That was correct.

Louisa asks about Stephen's promise to Rachael—It seemed, Louisa continued further, that Stephen's sufferings were the result of a promise he had made to Rachael to not become as the others. At this point, Rachael broke down and wept. Never had she intended to be the source of pain and hardship for Stephen, but she also knew that he would never allow himself to break his promise. Stephen, who had been listening in his earnest, attentive way, now interjected, explaining the deep honor and respect that he had for Rachael, whom he called his Angel and that it was true that he would never break his promise.

Louisa asks Stephen about his plans and offers him a bank note—Turning toward him with a newly found sense of respect and a softness in a her manner and voice, Louisa asked him what he planned to do now. Stephen smiled and said that he would simply make the best of his lot. Louisa then asked him how he planned to travel. He answered that he would go on foot. With that, she self-consciously took out a small purse, and removing a bank note from it, she laid it on the table with the request that Rachael somehow convince Stephen to take it. Rachael declined, however, gently informing Louisa that even she could not persuade Stephen to do anything that was not in his heart to do.

Overwhelmed by her kindness, Stephen accepts only a fraction and insists on repaying it—Overwhelmed, Stephen covered his face with his hand, and once he had recovered enough to remove it, he explained that no one, not even Rachael, could improve upon such a kind offer. He would gratefully accept two pounds worth (a much lesser sum), which he would work to repay, and it would be the sweetest labor he would ever have the privilege of applying himself toward. Dickens notes here that, despite Old Stephen's homely appearance, the level of graciousness he exhibited in that moment simply could not be taught.

Tom privately asks Stephen to wait for him outside the bank—Tom, who had been sitting on the bed watching and listening to the conversation, then asks Stephen whether he could have a private word with him in the hall. Once they are alone, he mentions to Stephen that he might be able to do some unspecified favor for him. When, he wants to know, is Stephen leaving? By the end of the week (this being Monday), comes the answer. Well, then, could he wait outside the bank for about an hour every day—not that Tom could make any promises since he was unsure whether he would be able to implement his idea. Stephen should, therefore, be discreet and not necessarily expect anything, but he should be ready. There was a possibility that he would be sending Bitzer with a note. On his way home, Tom would mention the matter to his sister, and he was sure she would approve. Following that, Tom left with his sister Louisa.

Mrs. Pegler is touched by Louisa's loveliness; Stephen and Rachael say goodbye—Deeply moved by Louisa Bounderby's loveliness, Mrs. Pegler could not help but break down and weep. However, she quickly contained herself lest any unexpected guests should arrive or return. It was also time to go home, so Stephen walked her and Rachael to their respective places—first, to drop off Mrs. Pegler at the Travelers' Coffee House and then to Rachael's usual turning-off point. He wanted to try to see Rachael again, but she thought it would be better if they cut things off then and there, not because of his recent trouble with his co-workers but because of their prior agreement. He promised to write and let her know what happened, and they left each other with their mutual blessings. Despite the hurry and the ordinary setting, Dickens emphasizes the sacred nature of their final parting and the blessings that these two ordinary people bestowed upon each other.

Stephen fulfills his work duties and waits daily by the bank—Stephen worked for several days after that, till his loom was bare, and every day, as agreed, he waited by the bank for over an hour. On the third and final night, he decided to play it safe and wait for two full hours. He could see Mrs. Sparsit in the window, and occasionally Bitzer would emerge from the bank. Stephen did his best to look occupied, but after an hour of striking various poses, he began to feel like a vagrant.

Dickens's descriptive rendering of Stephen's final hour outside the bank—As evening descends upon Coketown, the lamplighter appears to light the city's lanterns. The blinds on the first floor of the bank, where Mrs. Sparsit takes her tea, are let down. Dickens makes the most of his descriptive powers in this section, depicting, for example, the shadows of the lampposts as they merge together or the slight movement of the second-floor blinds as Mrs. Sparsit and Bitzer peek out on either side. Finally, when the two hours were done, Stephen let himself leave, relieved to be free of the situation.

Stephen leaves Coketown—Once home, he bid his landlady farewell, since he intended to leave in the earliest hours of the morning, before anyone else was about. At dawn, he took his bundle and went out into the empty streets. Here again, Dickens uses his descriptive powers to lead us out of the town through Stephen's eyes. As the pale sun rises over the deserted streets, he takes us past Rachael's place; past the factories, still quiet before the humdrum of the day's labor has begun; past the railroad and the brick villas; down the besmirched pathways till he reaches the hilltop. By then, the day has fully risen over the town, and Coketown is beginning to awaken. The beautiful final paragraph of this chapter describes the strangeness felt by Stephen as he turns from the dust and the grit and the red brick toward the birds and the trees and the open road, whose rustling leaves speak softly of a true love left behind.

Chapter 7—Gunpowder

Mr. Harthouse's jadedness—It was not difficult for Mr. Harthouse to earn points with the factual group, since his own philosophy was not that different from theirs. In his view, so-called philanthropists were hypocrites, the only difference being that they voiced opinions they didn't mean. He was not shy about voicing his own jaded opinions to Louisa Bounderby, and she, who had long grown accustomed to squashing her nobler yearnings and ideas, now listened with some degree of relief. She had long ago learned that there was no point in caring, since doing so would lead nowhere. As far as Mr. Harthouse was concerned, it had never occurred to him to truly care about anything, so he carried on, as always, in his own lackadaisical way.

Mr. Bounderby's country home and his lax attitude toward Louisa and Harthouse—Mr. Bounderby's home, situated some fifteen miles outside the town, had once belonged to one of Coketown's wealthier inhabitants. That person, Mr. Nickits had overshot his luck and was forced to foreclose on his house. That, of course, was a stroke of luck for Mr. Bounderby, who took over what could be described as a country manor, complete with elegant furniture and paintings, a flower garden and pond, and stables. In his usual blustering manner, he enjoyed comparing his own shabby background to the luxurious surroundings in which he now found himself. Nor did he seem to mind that Mr. Harthouse spent a fantastic deal of time at his home in the company of his young and pretty wife. He even encouraged him to make himself at home by bringing his horses, and he encouraged his wife to spend her time with highborn persons if that gave her pleasure.

Harthouse questions Louisa about Tom—In fact, there was one thing James Harthouse did care about, and that was the expression on Louisa Bounderby's face, which so far had only adjusted itself in a positive way for Tom, who, being selfish and reckless, barely deserved the honor. Mr. Harthouse's goal was to see if he could maneuver a change within Louisa Bounderby so that she might light up for him the way she did for her "whelp" of a brother. It was, therefore, no coincidence that James Harthouse "accidentally" came across Louisa Bounderby sitting in the woods near some trees that had been chopped down, watching the leaves of yesteryear. As he sat down next to her, he opened the conversation by mentioning her brother's name. Immediately, she lit up, prompting Harthouse to comment on how beautiful her expressions of sisterly love were. He excused himself for his frank admiration while she calmly waited for him to return to the subject of her brother. Finally, he got to the point: her brother's recklessness and lack of consideration were not surprising for his age. Did she think he gambled? Yes, was the reluctant reply. Feeling that the entire reply had not been forthcoming, Harthouse frankly stated that he thought Tom might be getting himself into trouble. Louisa, who found the conversation troubling and embarrassing, replied that she had already been aware of her brother's debts by the time she married and had shouldered them to some extent by selling some things of hers (evidently some of the gifts her husband gave her). She confessed to Harthouse that Tom had owed as much as one hundred pounds (back then the equivalent of $40,000) at a time. Harthouse added that he thought Tom owed it to her to be a better brother, with a greater display of gratitude than he commonly demonstrated, particularly in view of her selfless behavior towards him. This carelessness of his was, in Harthouse's opinion, no small offense.

Louisa and Harthouse meet Tom in the woods—This statement of Harthouse's evoked from Louisa some long and deeply hidden tears. Harthouse then explained his intention to correct her brother's faults. Having been through similar, even worse experiences, he considered himself in a position to do that. But now, he noticed Tom among the trees, so he and Louisa walked over to meet him, surprising him as he tore the moss from the base of the trees. When Harthouse asked him whose name he was carving in the bark, Tom replied that he would happily carve anyone's name, no matter how ugly, as long as she was rich and willing to send her money his way. Harthouse noted that he was mercenary in his attitudes, to which Tom replied that everyone was mercenary … just ask his sister. Louisa asked him whether he had been able to prove that, and Tom irreverently answered that if the shoe fit, she should wear it. Harthouse tried to mitigate Tom's rudeness by reminding him of the private opinions he had expressed in relation to Louisa. Within a short while, she went into the house, leaving the two of them alone.

Tom's selfishness emerges—Once Louisa was gone, Tom confessed to Harthouse the dire straits he was in. He was convinced that his sister could have rescued him from his condition, but she hadn't. She could have ingratiated herself to Bounderby. After all, she married him for Tom's sake. Instead, she sits there like a statue, unwilling to do what she needs to in order to get the money. To Tom, this made no sense.

Harthouse offers to help Tom but insists on kinder behavior toward Louisa—Disgusted with Tom's attitude, Harthouse had to resist the urge he felt to push him into the pond beneath them. Instead, he contained himself and offered to be his banker. At the mention of the word "banker," Tom turned white and insisted that they refrain from mentioning anything related to the subject. Resisting the temptation to wonder at that statement, Harthouse asked Tom to specify exactly how much he needed. Tom informed him that it was too late but that he was a "true friend" for asking. As Tom shook his hand, Harthouse thought to himself what an ass Tom was, but he nevertheless encouraged him to speak up when he was in trouble, since he might be able to show him a better way out. Harthouse, however, had one overriding request to make of Tom: it was critical, in his view, that Tom should kinder to his sister, and the time to start was now. This Tom did immediately, apologizing to Louisa for his earlier nasty behavior and showing his affection for her. The result of this was that Louisa smiled—and not just for Tom. Harthouse's plan was working.

Chapter 8—Explosion

Harthouse's self-satisfied amorality as he begins to gain Louisa's affection—Chapter 8 opens with James Harthouse contentedly sitting in the sunlit bay window of his dressing room as he reflects upon his recent conquest of Louisa Bounderby's heart. Here again, Dickens uses scene-painting as a way of creating an atmosphere that relates both to the setting and the character's state of mind. Old Stephen's departure from Coketown, as he turned from the smokestacks and the grime toward nature and the open road was another instance of the use of this technique. Now Dickens uses this sort of description to depict Harthouse's self-satisfaction as the smoke and fragrance from his exotic cigar wafts around him in the sunlight. There was no self-recrimination, no moral conflict—in fact, no specific plans at all as far as Louisa was concerned, though it seemed obvious enough where things would lead.

Dickens associates Harthouse with the Devil—By this point in the narrative, Dickens has associated Harthouse with the Devil several times, especially in his dealings with young Thomas Gradgrind, where he has given Harthouse a Mephistophelian role.[2] Here again, he explicitly mentions the Devil, saying that he is most dangerous when he is least obvious. When he takes the form of a "roaring lion," he is easy to spot and avoid; but when he is smooth and polished, when he has no strong opinions but seems to drift along aimlessly, then he is most dangerous. So it was with James Harthouse, who seemed barely aware of any deviousness on his part, and on arriving downstairs for breakfast, he was pleased to see that Louisa still entertained pleasant feelings toward him.

Bounderby tells Harthouse the bank has been robbed—That day, Harthouse had to attend to some business that would take him away from the house for the better part of the day. Returning at around six o'clock that evening, he was riding along the road leading to Bounderby's house, when Bounderby himself suddenly sprang out of the bushes, surprising his horse. "Have you heard?" he cried vehemently. Harthouse was at a loss as to what he meant, so Bounderby, standing right in front of his horse, burst out that the bank had been robbed the night before. The method had been strange: the robber had used a false key. When Harthouse asked how much had been taken, Bounderby was annoyed at the question. In his view, the principle was more crucial than the amount, which turned out to be not much more than a hundred and fifty pounds. But, Bounderby blustered, it could have been twenty thousand pounds—or twice that. At least, Mrs. Bounderby fainted on hearing the news,

---

[2] In the Faust legend, Faust sold his soul to Mephistopheles.

indicating that she knew how to react appropriately.

Details of the robbery—Louisa, Mrs. Sparsit, and Bitzer arrived just at that moment. Mrs. Sparsit would be staying with the Bounderbys for a few days to recover from the shock of having the bank robbed. Meanwhile, Harthouse inquired as to the details of the robbery. Bounderby impatiently replied that a small safe containing one hundred fifty-four pounds belonging to young Thomas Gradgrind had been broken into during the night and the bank door locked with a false key. "Where, by the way, was Tom?" asked Mr. Harthouse. The answer came that he was helping the police at the bank.

Old Stephen as the prime suspect—Harthouse then wanted to know whether there were any suspects. Of course, there were suspects, came the blustering reply; but Bounderby then became more secretive, asking that the information he was about to disclose should not be repeated. The suspicion was that a Hand had done it—yes, Stephen Blackpool was the suspect, and with good reason. Mr. Bounderby had all sorts of rationalizations as to why Blackpool made a good target, despite protests from Mrs. Bounderby and Mr. Harthouse, who found it difficult to believe that he would be capable of such an act. Bounderby, however, was thoroughly prepared with his elaborately constructed mythology about why a dissatisfied Hand would make a good suspect. Besides, hadn't Mr. Blackpool already tried to go against the established morality of the Church? And hadn't Bounderby himself told him that he would come to no good? Hadn't he also put poor Mrs. Sparsit, with her delicate sense of morality, into shock? Indeed, he had, she confirmed. And then, just like Bounderby's mother, he left town three days later—simply disappeared. But this Hand was even worse than Bounderby's mother because he was seen loitering around the bank every day before he left. Mrs. Sparsit and Bitzer had even seen him. And that wasn't all. There was an old woman who showed up periodically (here Bounderby had to embellish it a bit by saying that she flew in on her broomstick every so often) and would stand outside and watch for the entire day. When he said this, Louisa recalled the presence of the old woman at Stephen's that night and how she had hid in the shadows. Mr. Bounderby was convinced that there were more people involved, but he decided to hold his peace for the time being. Mr. Harthouse, too, had put in his two cents about the need for punishment and how without punishment, bank crimes would obviously multiply.

Mrs. Sparsit's idiosyncrasies emerge while she recovers at Bounderby's—In the meantime, Mrs. Sparsit would be given over to Mrs. Bounderby's care to make sure that she had every comfort. Though grateful for the consideration, Mrs. Sparsit insisted that she did not require a great deal of attention. In fact, she was so insistent in this respect that she came across as troublesome. She liked to remind people, especially when the servants were around, that her station in life was no longer what it had been. And she had to be persistently invited to eat the better dinner courses, and even then would insist on waiting for the simpler fare. Her most distinctive trait, however, was her obvious pity for Mr. Bounderby, which she would balance with a forced cheer to demonstrate her gratitude that he had managed to retain his good mood. Her other peculiarity, which she repeated many times a day, often apologizing when she did it, was that she could not bring herself to call Louisa by her married name but insisted on referring to her as "Miss Gradgrind."

Bounderby's mock trial and sentencing of Stephen; Mrs. Sparsit's efforts to cheer him—Dickens notes that following dinner, Bounderby held his own version of a trial, with the conclusion that the suspects were guilty and to be condemned according to the utmost legal punishment. After Bitzer was dispatched to send Tom home by mail train, Mrs. Sparsit attempted to cheer up Mr. Bounderby by recommending a game of backgammon, something he had given up due to Mrs. Bounderby's lack of interest. Mrs. Sparsit, however, would be happy to oblige, if he were willing.

Mrs. Sparsit's manipulation of Mr. Bounderby—From their seat by the window, they could just make out Louisa and Mr. Harthouse walking and talking in the garden. As Mrs. Sparsit repeatedly strained herself to see them more clearly, Mr. Bounderby asked her what was wrong—did she see a fire? No, she was concerned that Miss Gradgrind would catch cold from the dew. Bounderby dismissed the idea immediately, saying that she never caught a cold. That was hard to believe for Mrs. Sparsit, who felt compelled to fake a cough in response.

Before going to bed, Mrs. Sparsit noticed that Mr. Bounderby no longer took warm sherry with nutmeg and lemon peel. Instead, he had changed his habit to a simple glass of water before bedtime. Feeling that it would do him good, she offered to make it for him, toasting his health and happiness as she handed it to him. This was evidently all fine with "Miss Gradgrind," who let Mrs. Sparsit do as she pleased, thus allowing her deep empathy for poor Mr. Bounderby to shine to its full extent. Mr. Bounderby, for his part, knew that something felt strange about the whole scene, but he could not put his finger on its exact nature.

Louisa gently tries to get Tom to tell the truth—Over an hour past midnight, after finally hearing the bell ring at the mansion's gate, Louisa waited a few minutes, then rose out of her bed, put on a robe, and went upstairs to where her brother now lay in his bed. She walked silently over to him, and kneeling down, placed her face beside his. After a while, he pretended to wake up (having been awake the whole time), and asked her what was wrong. She gently asked him whether he had anything to tell her, but he replied that he didn't know what she was talking about. Again, she pleaded with him to tell her the truth, her long hair now covering him as though to hide him. Again, he claimed to be ignorant of what she was talking about. Louisa then conjured up the image of her death and implored him again, in the name of that time when she would be dead, to now tell her the truth. As he still feigned ignorance, she drew him to her breast and promised him that she would neither scold nor hurt him in any way; but still he refused to tell her anything and professed to not know what she meant.

Louisa questions Tom more directly but without luck—Resuming something more like her normal manner, she asked him whether, during the day's distractions, he had become aware of any news. Nothing she hadn't heard already from Bounderby. Louisa then wanted to know whether Tom had told anyone about their visit to Stephen's that night. He reminded her that she had made him promise not to tell anyone. She had not known at the time, she said, of what would happen at the bank. Neither had he, he quickly added. She now asked him whether he thought she should tell of their visit. Tom, in turn, was astonished that she was asking his advice, something she had never been in the habit of doing. His response was that whatever she chose to do, he would go along with it. Louisa then asked him whether he thought Stephen was guilty—he had seemed like such an honest man.

Tom avoids Louisa's questions, and once she's left, pours out his feelings on his pillow—Tom skirted the issue, saying that he couldn't see why he shouldn't be guilty that people might seem one way and be another. He then lied and said that the night of their visit, he had taken Stephen out into the hall to tell him what a splendid bonus he had received from his sister and that he hoped he would make the best of it. She asked whether Stephen had been offended, and Tom replied that he seemed to take it all right. After he kissed her good night, she asked him once more whether he didn't have anything to tell her. Again, the answer was no, this time embellished by the question of whether she would have him lie to her. No, she would not, especially not tonight, and she hoped that he would have many more, much happier nights in the future. He thanked her, told her to go to bed, kissed her again, and finally pulled his covers over his head. When he was sure that she had left the room, he quietly rose, bolted the door, and then, tossing himself down on his pillow, proceeded to cry, pull his hair, and pour out his confused feelings of reluctant love for his sister and his hatred for himself and for all good things.

Chapter 9—Hearing the Last of It

A rough transition for Mrs. Sparsit—The more we get to know Mrs. Sparsit, the more obnoxious and hypocritical she seems. She takes great pride in appearing gentle, considerate, and courteous, especially toward Mr. Bounderby, but behind his back, she insults his portrait, calling him a "Noodle" and telling him that he deserves everything he's received. If this vehemence came from some strong moral compunction with regard to older men marrying younger women or some other failing of Mr. Bounderby's, her behavior might be excusable. But her true concern is herself. She specializes in irritating Mr. Bounderby's wounds, of which he is barely aware, as obviously as she can, and she refuses to acknowledge Louisa's position as the new mistress of the household. She repeatedly calls her either Miss Gradgrind, Mrs. Gradgrind, or Miss Bounderby, but never her actual married name. For all her attempts to be as obviously and "graciously" insulting as possible (for example, by making a small scene when she "yields" her place at the breakfast table to Louisa), nobody else seems to care about the niceties that she thinks are so important.

Dickens's method of character development—Dickens never analyzes his characters outright. Instead, he sets the scene and allows us to deduce what we can from the characters' behavior—from small actions and interactions. In Mrs. Sparsit's case, he has a habit of describing her from what must be her own point of view—her aristocratic eyebrows, her Roman nose, her pseudo-gracious manner. She is convinced of her superiority and has a strong dislike of anything that contradicts it. Thus, her support of Mr. Bounderby when he supports her self-image and her resentment when he does not.

Mrs. Sparsit's revenge—It was no coincidence that Mrs. Sparsit's overdone courtesies and false humility began to cause added strife between Mr. Bounderby and his wife, or at least they made their differences more obvious. That, of course, was the plan, and it led not only to a greater distance between the Bounderbys but an added closeness between Louisa and Harthouse. Mrs. Sparsit had Louisa exactly where she wanted her: on an almost imperceptibly slow but steady decline in moral values and ultimately, therefore, her peace of mind.

Louisa visits her dying mother—Midway through the chapter, Louisa received a message via Bitzer that her mother was ill—more ill than usual. She, therefore, made her way by train to Coketown and the home she once knew as her own but has neglected to visit for a long time. She had felt no reason to do so, since her memories of the place were of the destruction of any sense of childhood joy, wonder, or imagination. Now she returned, older, sadder, more hardened, to visit her dying mother.

Louisa's mother senses something more; evidence of Sissy's effect on the family—On entering the room where her mother lay propped on a couch, straining to demonstrate some semblance of life force, Louisa noticed that her younger sister Jane, though resembling her somewhat, was much happier at age twelve than she had ever been. Jane was uninhibited in her affection for Sissy Jupe, whose gentleness she mirrored to some extent and who had also had a distinct effect on Mrs. Gradgrind. As Louisa's mother struggled to pronounce her final thoughts, she said that in all the -ologies her children had ever learned, there was something missing, though she couldn't pinpoint what it was. Mr. Gradgrind, who now spent most of his time in London, was certainly of no help, since his philosophy never included it. But looking at Sissy reminded her of this indefinable thing, whatever it was.

Mrs. Gradgrind's final moments—For all the sorrow and hardness Louisa had acquired over time, she still retained a deep compassion as she leaned over her mother and listened intently, trying to make sense of her dying words. Responding to her request for a pen to write down her final thoughts for her husband, Louisa watched as her mother began to trace something on the paper, when her spirit for good.

Chapter 10—Mrs. Sparsit's Staircase

The unseen staircase of doom—Mrs. Sparsit's staircase, though inspired by the vision of Louisa Bounderby descending a real staircase, refers to Mrs. Sparsit's uncharitable wish for a decline in Louisa's morals and morale. Louisa had not found happiness by following her father's and husband's philosophy of facts; and now, between Mr. Harthouse's advances and Mrs. Sparsit's resentful hopes of undermining her, Louisa was walking a slow but certain path of undoing. Her strict regimen of focusing on facts had not prepared her for the type of underhanded onslaught she was now experiencing, though she was still unaware of it. Straightforward facts did not, after all, account for the sorts of ulterior motives and dishonest approach that were part of the standard daily operating procedure for Mrs. Sparsit, Mr. Harthouse, and Louisa's own brother, Tom. Beneath her relatively composed, disciplined exterior, Louisa was still an innocent in a den of thieves, liars, and destroyers, though they appeared ever so smooth and proper on the surface. Their selfish interests were always their first concern, and they justified their selfishness by their belief that everyone thought and behaved as they did.

Lies and manipulation at the Bounderby residence—When Mr. Harthouse proposed the idea to Louisa that Old Stephen was the culprit in the bank robbery, it seemed a perfectly reasonable assessment to him. His lack of moral structure made it hard for him to imagine that anyone might have a higher basis for living than the usual self-interest that motivated him and others around him. After all, he had been discussing the subject with Louisa's brother, Tom, who was the source of the idea. Louisa's own sense of Stephen's character contradicted Harthouse's statements, and both she and Harthouse knew on some level that Tom was neither trustworthy nor reliable in financial matters. The reader is, therefore, left to conclude that the different characters are playing each other: Tom is attempting to manipulate Harthouse; Harthouse is distracting Louisa; Louisa's love for Tom and favorable disposition toward Harthouse, coupled with her dislike of her husband, are weakening her otherwise clear view of the facts; and Mrs. Sparsit is watching the whole thing from her busybody perch. This was helped along by Mr. Bounderby's complete ignorance of her hypocrisy so that, still convinced that she was an honorable and dignified lady, he allowed her to first extend her stay and then invited her to regularly spend the weekends at his residence while the weather was still good.

Bounderby's delusional beliefs feed the confusion—Matters with regard to Old Stephen were not helped by the fact that Bounderby himself believed him and Mrs. Pegler to be the guilty parties in the bank robbery. Bounderby, too, was being played by Tom, who was lying low and working harder than usual for the moment. Not being a psychologist, Bounderby never imagined that things might not be as they seemed. After all, this scenario perfectly suited his notion that every Hand wanted nothing less than a silver spoon in his mouth.

Louisa's invisible descent—So when Louisa found herself accosted by Harthouse, who secretly tried to convince her that her own good perception of Stephen was naïve and that she would do well to listen to his worldly wisdom and better knowledge of human nature, was it any wonder that she began to capitulate? His philosophy seemed to her a relief, maybe because it more closely matched her father's training than her own perceptions, which contradicted it. Yet she was honest enough to admit that something about her desire to believe Harthouse didn't seem quite right to her, although she could neither understand nor justify her doubts. With no support for truthfulness and clarity, unbeknownst to herself, she continued to slowly but surely slide down Mrs. Sparsit's staircase.

Chapter 11—Lower and Lower

Life continues as it is—So life went on in Coketown and beyond. Mr. Gradgrind buried his wife in a perfunctory manner and then returned to his parliamentary obligations. Mrs. Sparsit continued to watch Louisa descend her moral staircase, wishing her ill all the while, though she had to do this indirectly and from a distance, through her observations of letters, parcels, and other people's statements and observations. Mr. Harthouse continued trying to unravel the mystery of Louisa's reserve, without success. And Mr. Bounderby continued oblivious as ever to the two-faced maneuverings that surrounded him.

Mrs. Sparsit invites Tom to dinner to milk him for information about Harthouse—One day, when Mr. Bounderby was required to leave town for a few days, Mrs. Sparsit invited Tom up for lamb chops and ale after the bank closed. Being always ready to accept that sort of invitation, Tom easily agreed. Of course, Mrs. Sparsit had an ulterior motive: she wanted to know how Mr. Harthouse was doing. It turned out, according to Tom, that he was hunting and that he was quite good at it, as well. Professing him to be one of her favorite people, she next wanted to know when he would be returning. Tomorrow morning came the answer. He and Tom would be meeting in the evening, and though he wasn't expected at Bounderby's country estate, Tom would not put it past him to appear there. Throughout the meal, Tom had displayed his usual lack of manners, barely looking at Mrs. Sparsit, and when she asked him to deliver the message to Louisa that she would not be spending the weekend at Bounderby's, Tom grudgingly agreed, though he informed her that it was hardly worth the bother. Louisa, he said, completely unaware of the extent of his rudeness, never thought of Mrs. Sparsit anyway unless faced with her. Thus, having finished his meal and insulted Mrs. Sparsit, he excused himself and left.

Mrs. Sparsit secretly follows Tom and figures out Harthouse's plan—The following day, Mrs. Sparsit made it a point to be at the station that evening, although she tried to be as unobtrusive as possible. She watched in secret as Tom waited for Mr. Harthouse to arrive by train, but when he failed to keep his appointment while Tom restlessly waited, it dawned on her that the evening meeting between them had been a deliberate ploy. The idea was to keep Tom away from Stone Lodge, where Harthouse himself would be meeting Louisa.

Mrs. Sparsit quickly makes her way to Stone Lodge, where she confirms her suspicions—As soon as Mrs. Sparsit realized that, she leapt onto the next train and made her way to Stone Lodge as quickly and quietly as she could, convinced that she was about to witness Louisa's final fall into the dark pit that lay at the bottom her imagined moral staircase. Her secretive efforts were repaid when, after making her way past the gate and through the bushes, she finally saw Louisa and Harthouse by the felled log in the woods. She had been right. The meeting at the station had been a decoy to distract Tom so that Harthouse could be alone with Louisa.

Mrs. Sparsit witnesses Harthouse passionately courting Louisa—As Mrs. Sparsit came nearer, she could see and hear Harthouse, with his arm around Louisa, addressing her as his "dearest love" and claiming that he could not resist the temptation to meet her there, knowing that she was alone. He, too, had come in secret, taking his horse by a different route from the main road. Unable to look at him, Louisa hung her head. That prompted Mrs. Sparsit to resentfully mutter that Louisa was trying to make herself appear more attractive, even though Mrs. Sparsit herself could not see what others saw in Louisa to begin with.

Louisa rejects Harthouse's advances—Unfortunately for Harthouse, Louisa did not look favorably on his proposal to be with her. Not only would she not look at him—she even ordered him to leave, prompting him to call himself her ill-used yet devoted slave. It didn't matter to her: she would not hear of his staying there under any pretext.

Harthouse professes his love for Louisa but obeys her orders to leave—Mrs. Sparsit, whom Dickens describes as greedily watching and listening, then saw Mr. Harthouse put his arm around Louisa as he told her how much he loved her; how until then he had thought himself unable to love as he now did. Yet to his dismay he now found himself with the misfortune of being spurned by the object of his love, next to whom everything else paled in significance. Still, he acknowledged that he must obey her orders, and so he departed with his horse.

Mrs. Sparsit mistakes what she sees and follows Louisa to catch her in the act—In the meantime, it had begun to rain, making it even more difficult for Mrs. Sparsit to decipher the hushed conversation between Louisa and Harthouse. All she knew—she thought—was that they would be meeting later that evening and that she must, therefore, track Louisa carefully to see where she went. By now, it was raining heavily, and Mrs. Sparsit no longer looked the part of the sedate, highborn lady as she stealthily followed Louisa to the station. Dripping wet and covered with caterpillars and other bits of nature, she hid herself under her shawl to ensure that she would not be recognized. In this condition, she bought her ticket, sat in a separate corner of the waiting room, and finally boarded a separate car from the one chosen by Louisa.

Mrs. Sparsit loses Louisa in the thunderstorm—By now, the rain was pouring. There were peals of thunder and flashes of lightning, as though to suggest an external parallel for the drama of internal events now unfolding. Dickens describes the train as shrieking along until it finally pulls into Coketown. Mrs. Sparsit had figured that Louisa would go from the train to a carriage, so her goal was to track which one she entered amidst the flurry of activity. But she was wrong! Louisa was nowhere in sight, and as Mrs. Sparsit floundered around trying to discover what had happened to her, she finally realized to her tearful, bitter dismay that she had lost her.

Chapter 12—Down

Louisa enters her father's study in disarray—Mr. Gradgrind, on vacation from his parliamentary duties, sat at the desk in his study, engrossed in solving some factual problem. Occasionally, he would note the thunder and lightning outside his window, but for the most part, he did not think about it too much except to wonder whether Coketown's buildings had been affected. While he was thus occupied, the door to the study opened to reveal Louisa standing before him, drenched and almost unrecognizable in her state of distress. As she unceremoniously dropped her soaking cloak on the ground, she informed her father that she wanted to speak with him, and it was clear from her wild, disheveled appearance that the situation was urgent.

Mr. Gradgrind's compassion for his beloved daughter—Mr. Gradgrind may have held a firm conviction of the value of facts and factualness, but he was not a coldhearted person, and the sight of his eldest daughter in this sorry state upset him as much as it would any loving father. This was, after all, his pride and joy—the perfect result of his carefully thought-out system—now standing before him, an unexpected, illogical wreck.

Louisa expresses her long repressed thoughts and feelings—Louisa had not yet completely lost her composure, but now, for the first time in her life, she began to bare all the repressed thoughts and feeling that had never fit into the system so carefully laid out by her father. Worse, she revealed the sense of misery that had plagued her for so long—the sense that something vital was missing, squashed before it even had a chance to live. To her, her life seemed nothing more than a living death, a grey existence that might have been salvaged if the seeds of imagination and wonder had been allowed to grow instead of being routed out by the tyranny of fact and calculation.

Mr. Gradgrind listens with dismay to Louisa's discouraging statements—Mr. Gradgrind listened to his daughter and acknowledged what she was saying, though with difficulty. Even in her distress, she could hold herself together enough that she was able to deliver her message in an organized, eloquent manner. But the message itself was disheartening, if not frightening: it questioned the basis of everything her father had built his life upon, the foundation of his children's education. Everything he had ever held dear he now discovered to be the source of misery for the triumph of his educational efforts—his daughter Louisa. That child now wanted to know whether he would have made the same choices or encouraged the same behavior if he had known how unhappy they made her.

Love: the missing ingredient in the philosophy of facts—One of Dickens's strengths is that he makes his points clear without ever stating them directly. As in the scene with her dying mother, Louisa's interaction with her father is obviously about love, the primary factor that is missing from the Gradgrind philosophy. Yet it's clear throughout this scene that Louisa and her father love each other: he thought all along that he was ensuring her a good future, and she did her best to obey to him. But his calculations were wrong, and her obedience led to unhappiness. Now she wanted to know whether her happiness was more important to him than his philosophy. Would he have forced his philosophy on her if he had understood the effect it was having? His warm and tender answer was "no."

Louisa desperately seeks the answer to her distress—From their interaction and from a previous conversation with Tom, it's clear that Louisa knew her father's character before she asked the question. It was not her father she was at odds with but his philosophy. In fact, in this scene, Louisa acts as a mouthpiece for all that is wrong with the Gradgrind-Bounderby approach to life. Because she is to some extent the product of that approach, she can pinpoint what is missing but does not yet know how to fix her desperate situation. Now she reaches out to her father, the source of the philosophy, on the off chance that he can help her find the answer.

Louisa reveals the conflict aroused by her miserable marriage and Harthouse's passion—The misery resulting from her father's philosophy was only the precursor to the main subject Louisa had come to address—her unhappy marriage, which was now being threatened in a way that neither she nor her father had ever imagined. She first asserts that she never would have chosen to marry Bounderby if her mind and heart had not been as deadened as they were at the time she received the proposal. Even then, her motivation to go ahead with it was love—not for her husband-to-be but for her brother, who requested her companionship. That would have all been fine, except for the arrival of Mr. James Harthouse, whose obvious interest in her awakened a smoldering passion that, though barely alive, still had not been extinguished by all the deadening facts, logic, and discipline that had been the hallmarks of her life. The problem was that she was unprepared for this awakening within herself and for Harthouse's utter lack of moral structure, though she did not fault him but recognized some of that mentality in herself. The sleeping giant of her passion, fire, and imagination had now begun to stir and was threatening the shaky foundations of her life, leaving her weak, distressed, and desperate, unable to fight herself anymore. Now, with her husband out of town and Harthouse professing his passionate love, she had reached her breaking point. She had not succumbed, but the power of her feelings left her questioning her own morality and reaching out for something beyond the philosophy she had been raised on. Dismayed, her father lovingly held her in his arms, supporting her in her weakness until she cried out that she could bear it no longer and to let her fall to the ground.

BOOK III: GARNERING

Chapter 1—Another Thing Needful

Louisa awakens in her old bed—The next morning, Louis awoke, still dazed and weak, to find herself in the room and bed she used to call her own. Eventually, all that had gone on between her younger days and now came back to her, as what momentarily had seemed like a dream reverted to reality. She gradually noticed that her sister Jane was sitting next to her, shyly holding her hand. When had she been brought there, she wanted know, and who had brought her? Jane believed it had been Sissy who brought her there the night before because this morning she had found Sissy sitting next to the bed cooling Louisa's forehead. She had left Jane with the instructions to tell their father when Louisa awoke.

Louisa wrestles with mixed feelings—As Jane shyly bent over to kiss her older sister, Louisa couldn't help noticing how happy she looked. Her younger sister hadn't been aware of it but guessed that it had something to do with Sissy. On hearing that, Louisa withdrew her arm from Jane's neck and told her that she could call their father. Louisa then asked whether Jane had been responsible for the cheeriness of the room, but when Jane implied that it had been Sissy, Louisa again turned away.

Dickens's archetypal use of characters—Here Dickens uses his characters in an archetypal way, as he so often does. Sissy represents the pure innocence of love, while Louisa represents the jaded human soul, struggling to recognize its original self but finding it hard to break free from the layers of sadness, resentment, and deadening that have nearly crushed it out of existence. Her sense of self has been built on other premises, and she, therefore, repeatedly turns away from love out of confusion.

Louisa's father seeks forgiveness and understanding—In the meantime, Jane had gone to fetch their father, who now anxiously entered the room to check on his beloved daughter. His manner was tender and solicitous, and it was clear that his eldest daughter's state was deeply troubling to him. In fact, he could barely bring himself to say what he now had to say. Finally, he confessed that the foundation that had always seemed so stable to him—his life's work—now stood on shaky ground. Yet he could not guarantee that, had his philosophy been questioned earlier, his reaction would have been more useful or flexible. He knew that he had taken a rigid approach, and he was ready to accept the blame for its failures. All he asked of his beloved Louisa was that she would understand that his intentions had been good.

Gradgrind questions his philosophy and his perceptive ability—Louisa assured him that she understood and did not blame him. As he tenderly held her hand, he told her that he had spent all night in his study thinking about the implications of the previous evening's events. He had concluded that if she had managed to hide such passionate feelings from him for such a long time, he could no longer trust himself. He followed his statement by gently stroking her hair, the type of action that took on added significance in his case because it was so rare. The problem, he continued, was that if he was untrustworthy in such matters, how could he respond adequately to her call for help?

Mr. Gradgrind wonders about the validity of the heart's wisdom—Still lying down, Louisa now turned away from her father so that he was unable to see her face. Still uncertain, he continued. There were some people, he said, who held that the heart had its own particular wisdom, apart from the head. He had always thought that the wisdom of the head was enough, but now he had his doubts. Now he wondered whether the wisdom of the heart was not the missing factor in his system. It had occurred to him that his frequent absences from home might have had a beneficial effect on Louisa's younger sister, who, though she was raised according to the regular system, also had other influences. Mr. Gradgrind now humbly asked his daughter for her opinion on the subject. Still looking away, Louisa answered that if Jane had inadvertently come upon a happier, more harmonious way of being than she herself had experienced, then this should be considered an influential blessing.

Mr. Gradgrind begins to recognize the power of love—At this point, her father could not contain his remorse at her unhappiness. He then made a further confession: it seemed to him that while the wisdom of the head had neglected to do what it could not, in fact, do, the heart had been secretly and gradually working its effect, simply through gratitude and love. Now he wondered whether this could indeed be so. He was rational and humble enough to question his own philosophy and to acknowledge its undeniable failure in the case of his eldest daughter.

Mr. Gradgrind leaves, and Sissy enters the room—Louisa made no answer, so her father quietly left the room. Shortly afterwards, Louisa heard another lighter footstep and sensed a presence beside her. At first, she was angry and resentful at being seen in her current state. Her emotions had been pent up for so long that she now had difficulty expressing them. But when she felt a gentle touch, her thoughts began to soften, and she soon became aware that the tears in her own eyes were mingling with the tears of another, whose face now touched hers.

Sissy's offer of love—Seeing Louisa move, Sissy backed off a bit. Louisa then asked why she was spending time with her when she should be with her sister, who thought the world of her. Sissy responded that she would like to be the same thing for Louisa, if she would let her. She knew that Louisa had had mixed feelings about her for a long time, and she wasn't hurt by it. She understood the change that took place after Bounderby's marriage proposal. But she had always loved Louisa, and now she wanted to be whatever she could for her.

Louisa confesses the sad, hard state of her soul and questions the extent of Sissy's love—When Sissy asked if she could try, Louisa took her hand and asked her whether she truly understood the extent of her resentment, hardheartedness, and confusion. Did that not bother her? No! came the decided reply. Louisa continued, pouring out the misery of her soul and confessing that if she had only had less factual knowledge and a greater understanding of life's simple truths, she would have been a happier, better, more peaceful person. Again, she wanted to know whether that didn't bother Sissy, and again she received the same reply: No!

The healing, leveling power of love—Dickens describes Sissy as beaming the light of her loving soul upon Louisa's darkened state of mind. Kneeling down before Sissy, Louisa hugged her tightly, and looking up respectfully, she pleaded for forgiveness and compassion and the chance to lay her troubled head upon a heart full of love. Dickens's emphasis here is the turning of the tables. He refers to Sissy as the "stroller's child," the lowest of the low, who now raises up one of Coketown's leading ladies with a heart of pure love.

Chapter 2—Very Ridiculous

Harthouse is in a frenzy over Louisa's rejection and disappearance—Louisa's refusal and sudden disappearance had Mr. Harthouse in such a frenzy for the next twenty-four hours that he was practically unrecognizable. He had accused the porter of failing to deliver his messages; gone looking for Louisa at Bounderby's Coketown residence and the bank; and even interviewed Tom to find out what he knew, which was nothing useful. The situation left him frustrated and baffled, especially since he felt that his fate hinged on its meaning. That meant that he spent a fair bit of time trying to determine whether he had moved too soon, whether they had been found out or she had lost heart, or whether he and her husband would have to fight it out. This last concept led him to ruminate about what that might entail—whether to train, for example, or hire someone else to do the work.

Sissy Jupe confronts Harthouse—As the day dragged on, Harthouse found himself pacing the floor of his hotel room and watching out for any sign of communication. By nighttime, as he was finally settling down with some candles and a newspaper, the hotel waiter arrived with a strange message that a young lady had come and was waiting outside the door to see him. Harthouse quickly went out into the hall to see who it was and noticed a remarkably pretty young woman with a remarkably innocent yet serious and fearless air about her. It was, of course, Sissy Jupe, and once she had verified that she was indeed speaking with Mr. Harthouse, she immediately launched into the purpose of her visit. He had already been caught off guard by the combination of her strength and innocence, and when she began to speak of assurances of honor on his part as a gentleman, he became even more uncomfortable, but quickly gave her his word. Next she told him that she was there entirely of her own volition, which struck Harthouse as particularly strong but baffled him at the same time. He could not determine the intention of her visit, though he could see that her motives were selfless. When she told him that Louisa was at her father's house, he became even more confused. Sissy, however, explained the sequence of events and then pointedly informed Harthouse that he could expect with certainty to never see Louisa again.

Harthouse is unable to resist her demand—Perhaps for the first time in his life, Mr. Harthouse found himself at a loss for words, completely unprepared for the type of person he was now dealing with and the level of her conviction. Finally, he asked Sissy whether the message had originated with Louisa (whose name they never actually mentioned). When the answer came back as "no," he thought for a moment that he might have a chance at salvaging the situation. But Sissy was firm. Her decision rested on a deep sense of love and morality that Harthouse could only imagine and against which he found himself powerless. Dickens is funny in his description of Harthouse's response to Sissy when she informs him that the authority for her actions rests exclusively on her love, trust, and understanding of Louisa's character. Instead of saying that his heart was moved, Dickens describes it as "the cavity where his heart should have been"—the type of detail that makes his writing so memorable.

Harthouse admits he is to blame and takes responsibility—One of the effects of Sissy's character on James Harthouse was that it made him more honest, to the extent that that was possible. As he struggled to articulate what was going on in his mind, he openly admitted his lack of morality, but at the same time, he was becoming aware that he had unconsciously done a considerable amount of damage and that he had to agree with Sissy (though he didn't want to) that seeing Louisa was probably no longer an option. He did not see himself ever adopting a code of morality, but he was ready to admit his mistake and accept the blame.

Sissy's final demand—Looking at Sissy, Harthouse realized that she had something else to say, so he asked her about it. Firmly but gently, she informed him that his only chance for repairing the damage he had done was to leave town immediately and permanently. Their present conversation would remain strictly between them, and though she had no authority for her demand other than her own love and conviction, she also had no doubts.

Harthouse sees it all as ridiculous—Floored again by her request, Mr. Harthouse asked her whether she understood the magnitude and context of what she was demanding. He had made a commitment to a public business, and his sudden leaving would create a significant effect. Furthermore, he said, as he paced the room, the entire situation was ridiculous.

None of that mattered to her, and she stuck to her demand. She was absolutely convinced that this was the only possible route. He realized that he had no choice but to agree, so he confirmed that their meeting would be kept confidential. Still, the whole thing seemed ridiculous to him.

Harthouse asks the name of his "enemy"—As Sissy stood up to leave, her bright face convey her obvious satisfaction with her accomplishment. Harthouse felt obliged at that moment to tell her that he did not think that any other person could have succeeded in persuading him the way she had. He then asked for the "privilege" of learning the name of the "enemy" who had so totally conquered him.

At first surprised by the question, she told him her name. He asked her whether she was a relation of the family. No, came the answer, she was just "a poor girl," a stroller's child who had been taken in by the family out of pity when her father abandoned her. Having explained that, Sissy departed.

Harthouse leaves Coketown for good—The simple fact of her poverty and her originally low station in life left Mr. Harthouse feeling even more ridiculous. How could someone so simple and lowly conquer, with so little effort, a worldly man like James Harthouse? Here again, Dickens displays his capacity for humor. Harthouse referred to himself as "a Great Pyramid of failure," and in the next sentence, the "Great Pyramid" decided to make Egypt his next destination. He hastily composed several notes, the first being to his brother, Jack, to inform him of his move. Though it was already late, he called to have the porter awoken in order to start packing, and after writing several more notes to Bounderby and Gradgrind announcing his retirement and departure, Mr. James Harthouse boarded the next train out of Coketown and was gone forever.

A perpetually amoral man—Dickens closes the chapter with a few wondering remarks about Mr. Harthouse's hopeless amorality. A moral person, he muses, might imagine that Harthouse had improved his moral sense and learned a valuable lesson. He might even have experienced a feeling of relief and gratitude on doing the right thing, for a change, and fleeing an even worse situation. But Mr. Harthouse did not think that way. He was more concerned with the opinions of other worldly men, and what should have relieved his conscience (if he'd had one) instead shamed his vanity.

Chapter 3—Very Decided

Bounderby drags Mrs. Sparsit to Stone Lodge to confront Mr. Gradgrind—So far, Book 3 has been about the full flowering of each character's personality and deeds. We have already seen the results of Mr. Harthouse's complete lack of moral structure, and now Mrs. Sparsit and Mr. Bounderby manifest their characters in full. Mrs. Sparsit's pettiness, pretentiousness, and vindictiveness blossomed when, sopping wet and adorned with thistles and caterpillars, she sought out Mr. Bounderby in the city to tell him the supposed news that his wife had abandoned him for another man. Even worse, her pretense of honor and propriety masked her own selfish ends. For her trouble, she caught a horrific cold, which left her barely able to speak when Bounderby, having dragged her with him late at night to confront Louisa's father, called upon her to announce her findings.

On learning the truth of Louisa's whereabouts, Bounderby sends Mrs. Sparsit home—Since Mrs. Sparsit's hoarse voice and faint, wretched condition left her unable to make more of a mess at this point than she already had, Mr. Bounderby had to address the situation himself in his usual blustering and inflated manner. Feeling that he had been betrayed by his young wife, whom he now deemed unworthy of him, he displayed an even more obnoxious, self-congratulatory, and intolerant demeanor than usual. It took Mr. Gradgrind repeated attempts before he could persuade Bounderby to listen. Gradgrind had sent Bounderby a letter informing him of Louisa's current whereabouts and condition, but Bounderby had missed it. On discovering that Louisa was there, he turned to Mrs. Sparsit for an apology, but at that point Mrs. Sparsit could do nothing more than weep. Bounderby's reaction was to put her in a coach and send to her residence at the bank, with the instructions to drink some rum and soak her feet in hot water.

Bounderby is in a particularly obnoxious mood—Bounderby having now returned to Mr. Gradgrind's study, the two men continued their previous conversation. Josiah Bounderby of Coketown, it should be known, was in no mood to be contradicted. Furthermore, he did not want to be addressed politely (as "my dear Mr. Bounderby") nor would he ever be polite, as that was not his nature. If Mr. Gradgrind preferred politeness, he should associate instead with his "gentleman friends." By that, Gradgrind took him to mean Mr. Harthouse, though Bounderby flatly denied it.

Mr. Gradgrind tries to get Bounderby to soften his approach—Louisa's father had also already asked

Bounderby to tone down his volume for Louisa's sake, since she was trying to rest. But throughout the chapter—whether toward Louisa, Mrs. Sparsit, or Mr. Gradgrind himself—Bounderby showed no consideration for anyone but himself. Whatever qualities of charm or tolerance he previously displayed were now replaced by arrogance and impatience. Mr. Gradgrind now tried to convey that his understanding and education of Louisa had not been quite right, and he hoped that Bounderby would help him to set things right. Not knowing what he meant and still showing an intolerant, impatient approach, Bounderby declined to promise anything. Thomas Gradgrind, on the other hand, had softened considerably out of love for his favorite child. He had come to a point where he thought it would be best to allow her own nature to guide her for a while. For this, she would need the tender support and patience of her family.

Bounderby's ego gets the better of him, and he issues Louisa's father an ultimatum—Unfortunately, Bounderby's injured and swollen ego prevented him from taking a compassionate approach. In his rude and blunt way, with a wide stance, flushed face, and tousled hair, he informed Mr. Gradgrind of his stubborn opinion that Louisa now belonged to the ranks of those who cared for nothing less than turtle soup and silver spoons. Anything to do with emotion or imagination or a softening of the heart was unacceptable to him, and he refused to provide it. After all, Josiah Bounderby of Coketown deserved better than a wife who didn't know his worth. It was clear, that unlike Mrs. Sparsit, Louisa was not a high-born lady who could appreciate his finer qualities. He hypocritically added that he didn't care much for social status and then insulted Mr. Gradgrind by repeatedly referring to his daughter's lower social status. Gradgrind, who had been patiently putting up with Bounderby's rudeness and egocentricity, suggested it might be better for them to end the discussion for now. But Bounderby, who had repeatedly interrupted him, kept accusing Gradgrind of interrupting him and insisted on centering the conversation on his own needs. Even Gradgrind's appeals for kindness and honor with regard to the trust that Bounderby had taken on in marrying Louisa had no effect. The great magnate of Coketown had no sympathy for the idea that she needed time to recover before returning to her appropriate place. He concluded that he and Louisa were incompatible and that she was either to submissively return to their home by noon the next day, or her things would be packed and shipped to the Gradgrind residence. Mr. Gradgrind asked him to reconsider, but Josiah Bounderby of Coketown always made his decisions immediately. He would have nothing to do with emotional nonsense.

Bounderby separates from Louisa and puts the country house up for sale—With that, Mr. Bounderby left as unceremoniously as he had come. When noon arrived on the following day, Louisa's things were packed and sent to her, and the country house was put up for sale.

Chapter 4—Lost

Bounderby steps up his investigation of the bank robbery—Since Bounderby's ego always took first place, and since the success of his business ventures was critical in ensuring its ongoing inflatedness, he refused to allow his personal issues to interfere. He had never stopped investigating the bank robbery, but now he stepped up his efforts—to the dismay of the officers involved.

Bounderby plasters wanted posters about Stephen on Coketown's walls—In fact, no new progress had been made since the robbery first came to light, so Bounderby, to breathe new life into the investigation, had a large poster made listing all known details about Stephen Blackpool and his disappearance, and promising a large monetary reward. This was all printed on tabloid-sized sheets and plastered all over the walls of Coketown in the middle of the night so that its impact would be dramatic and widespread.

Slackbridge uses the poster situation to further defame Stephen's character—The posters had the desired effect, and even though many Coketown Hands could not read, they gathered around them with a great interest that would last throughout the work day. Slackbridge, the same man who had made the condemning speeches about Stephen Blackpool before Old Stephen left town, now unfolded the contents of the posters to the illiterate Hands, and he did so with the exaggerated eloquence and fervor of a revolutionary or religious leader. Reading the poster was not enough: he had to dramatize it, embellish it, and insert his own slant on the event and on Stephen's character, not to mention on the poster itself. A few people in the crowd had the presence of mind to contradict Slackbridge's exaggerated claims, but their numbers were nothing compared to the masses who bought his story and cheered him on.

Louisa is visited that evening by Bounderby, Tom, and Rachael—Later that evening, as the Hands returned home from their fifteen-hour work day, Louisa received a message from Sissy that she had visitors—Mr. Bounderby, her brother Tom, and a woman named Rachael, whom she supposedly knew and who looked angry and tearful. Louisa explained to her father that she had to receive them, so Sissy ushered them in, with Tom straggling reluctantly by the door.

Rachael tells her story and asks for confirmation from Louisa—Mr. Bounderby presented himself formally and politely to his wife and father-in-law. He even apologized for the lateness of the hour but explained that young Tom's refusal to confirm Rachael's claims had made it necessary. Rachael reminded Louisa that they had met before, which elicited a cough from Tom. When Louisa failed to respond, Rachael repeated her statement, which drew the same reaction from Tom. When Louisa confirmed it, Rachael reacted with a look of triumph toward Bounderby and then asked Louisa to divulge the details of the meeting. This she did, describing the place and the people who were there, including her brother and the old woman, who remained semi-hidden most of the time. On Rachael's request, she added her reason for the visit, namely, her desire to help Stephen. She had offered him a bank note, but he had only been willing to take two pounds.

Bounderby finally believes Rachael—Bounderby, who had considered Rachael's story ridiculous, promptly admitted (though not happily) that Louisa's version matched her own. Rachael then explained to Louisa what had happened with the poster and the town meeting, where Stephen's good and honest name had been blackened even more than before. She broke down crying, bitter with the injustice of it all.

Rachael expresses her doubts about Louisa's honesty, but Louisa is sympathetic—When Louisa expressed her sorrow at the situation, Rachael returned that she hoped her statement was true but that she couldn't be sure. The town's wealthy residents didn't understand or care about the poor working folk. At the time, both she and Stephen had been deeply grateful for Louisa's empathy, but now, with all the trouble it had caused Stephen, she couldn't be sure that there hadn't been some ulterior motive. Despite the untruth of her statement, Louisa sympathized and understood, but Tom, himself bitter and angry, scolded her.

Bounderby reminds Rachael of her original intention—After a few moments of listening to her soft sobbing, Mr. Bounderby reminded Rachael of her original intention in coming there. She explained that when she first saw the posters about Stephen, she immediately went to the bank to say that she knew Stephen's whereabouts and would ensure his return in a couple of days. When she finally found Mr. Bounderby later that evening, she informed him of everything she knew, but he chose to disbelieve her, which was why they were now at Stone Lodge for confirmation.

Rachael speaks of her letter to Stephen—Bounderby reminded Rachael again that she had come to do something specific and that she had better stop talking and get on with it. In response, Rachael said that she had sent Stephen a letter that afternoon, in addition to a previous letter she had sent him. She was sure that he would be back in Coketown within two days. Bounderby interjected that she couldn't be sure of that, since she, too, was under suspicion by virtue of her association with Stephen. For all they knew, her letter might never have reached him.

Focusing on Louisa, Rachael added that a week after his departure, Stephen had written her saying that he had had to change his name in order to get work. Bounderby's unsupportive comment was that that could only bode ill for Stephen, since name changes never looked good in court. Frustrated and unhappy, Rachael wondered what else he could have done when both the wealthy and the working classes were against him.

Rachael voices her full faith that Stephen will return to clear his name—Louisa again voiced her deep sorrow at the situation but added that she was sure that Stephen would clear himself. Agreeing, Rachael believed that Stephen would return on his own, not because he was pressured into it. She had full faith in him, regardless of other opinions. Bounderby was satisfied that Rachael's claims had proven true, so he excused himself for the night to further investigate the matter. He was followed by young Tom, who left with him, still grimacing and mostly keeping to himself.

Louisa assures Rachael of her trustworthiness; Sissy offers her help and support—Once they had left, Louisa gently informed Rachael that she would someday trust her when she got to know her better. Rachael apologized for her mistrust, adding that it wasn't her nature and that she did not truly believe what she had said about Louisa earlier. Yet with all the injustice done to Stephen, she could not promise that she wouldn't believe it again. Sissy asked Rachael if Stephen knew that his evenings spent near the bank were the reason for the suspicions. She thought the information might help him prepare his defense. Rachael answered that he was aware of it but added that she couldn't understand what had brought him there, since it was out of his usual way. After giving Sissy permission to check with her at home in the coming days, Rachael left.

Mr. Gradgrind realizes that Stephen's innocence implies another's guilt—Throughout the conversation, Mr. Gradgrind had listened silently. To his knowledge, he had never encountered Stephen, and now he wondered whether Louisa thought there was any truth in the accusations. She replied that she had thought so for a while, though without conviction, and now she no longer did. Listening to her assessment of Stephen's honesty and seeing Rachael's faith, Gradgrind concluded that he must not be the actual thief. Someone else was guilty—but who? and where was he? and did he know what was being done to Stephen?

Louisa comforts her father and motions to Sissy to keep silent about Tom—Looking at her father, Louisa noticed how he had aged, and quickly went to his side to sit with him. In itself, the action was small, but it spoke volumes about the tenderness in Louisa's character and her deep love for her father. Dickens hints that Sissy may have guessed the real thief in that moment, while Louisa was sitting next to her pondering father. Their eyes met, and noticing a change in Sissy's face, Louisa motioned to her, with her finger to her lips, to stay quiet. Following that, any updates about Stephen were transmitted in hushed tones, and the subject of the robbery was generally avoided.

Stephen's failure to show and young Tom's strange behavior—Four days later, when Stephen still hadn't arrived, Rachael guessed that he hadn't received her letter, so she visited the bank to give them his address at an out-of-the-way work colony. The bank sent messengers to the colony, and Stephen was expected to arrive with them at the station the next day, but he never showed. Young Tom, the "whelp," had predicted exactly this, and he waited at the station to confirm it. His own actions had lately been particularly nervous and feverish, and he followed Bounderby everywhere.

Stephen's disappearance—Apparently, Stephen had received Rachael's letter and had left the colony immediately. At this point, no one knew where he was, and half the town wondered whether Rachael had warned him to escape instead of asking him to return. A week or two later, when there was still no word of Stephen, young Tom started to make noise. If Stephen was innocent, why didn't he show himself? Where was he, anyway? Tom's own words haunted him throughout the night.

Chapter 5—Found

The ongoing mystery of Stephen's disappearance—The days passed, and still there was no sign of Stephen Blackpool. As time went on, his disappearance became just another part of Coketown's humdrum routine. Rachael continued believing and trusting in Stephen, though she felt there were precious few in Coketown who shared her faith in his goodness. Sissy kept visiting her every night, providing her hope and comfort and, according to Rachael, a way to stay sane. Even Rachael herself was somewhat suspected, yet Sissy remained faithful.

Rachael's suspicions of murder—Sissy firmly believed that Stephen would one day clear his name, and by her account, so did everyone at Stone Lodge. That was comforting to Rachael, and she now felt bad that she had ever openly mistrusted Louisa. But something still bothered her about the situation. The fact that Stephen still had not returned, when he was most likely innocent, seemed out of character and implied that he had gone missing for other reasons—possibly even murder. This was not something that Rachael said lightly. In fact, she said it in such a low voice that Sissy had to strain to hear her, and when she did take it in, she turned pale and shuddered. It occurred to Sissy that he might have gotten sick on the way to Coketown and stopped somewhere en route, but Rachael reminded her that all possible places had been checked, and no one had found him. Rachael had even sent him money in case he got tired of walking.

Sissy helps Rachael to clear her head—Like so many other scenes in *Hard Times*, this one, too, uses the scene's external circumstances as a metaphor for the characters' inner states. During this first part of the scene, Sissy and Rachael were sitting together in the dark in Rachael's small but clean apartment. The setting conveys a sense of isolation and mystery that matches the discussion. Earlier in the conversation, Rachael mentioned that the thoughts of murder had left her distressed, and she would need to walk them off before going to bed. When Sissy invited her out into the open air, it both opened up the environment and related back to giving Rachael a chance to release her disturbing thoughts. Sissy's goal was to keep Rachael as sane and healthy as possible, knowing that she might be needed to support Stephen in clearing himself. To do this, she was even willing to take time out on a Sunday to walk with Rachael in the fresh country air.

Mrs. Sparsit arrives by train with Mrs. Pegler in tow—Mr. Bounderby's Coketown residence was near the train station, and as Rachael and Sissy approached it, a train happened to be screeching into the station, causing quite a commotion. The coach had just come to a stop, when they noticed Mrs. Sparsit, who waved to them to stop. In an obvious frenzy, she hauled the old woman out of the train, informing all onlookers that they were not to interfere—that the old woman "belonged" to her. She was in a state of triumph, convinced that she had just taken great strides toward helping Mr. Bounderby unravel the mystery of the bank robbery. She managed to generate enough interest that the crowd of twenty-five people that had gathered around now followed her into the house. They were accompanied by Sissy and Rachael, who had been summoned by Mrs. Sparsit. The poor old woman had been dragged in by the throat as the spectators climbed onto Bounderby's dining room chairs to get a better look.

Mrs. Pegler reveals the truth about Bounderby's past—Still in a state of frenzy, Mrs. Sparsit yelled to have Mr. Bounderby called downstairs from his conference with both Mr. Gradgrind and his son Tom. Unfortunately, his reaction to her triumphant catch was not what she expected. He was not at all pleased with the crowd in his dining room, and when he saw Mrs. Pegler, his response was to scold Mrs. Sparsit for butting into his family affairs. It turned out that Mrs. Pegler was Josiah Bounderby's mother, and the truth of his background, which she now unfolded, was nothing like the lies upon which he had built his reputation. He had not been abandoned by his mother who, with his father, had raised him lovingly and unselfishly. His grandmother had not been an irresponsible, abusive drunk but had died before his birth. He had not been left to fend for himself in the gutter but had been taught to write beautifully, and after his father's death, he had been apprenticed to a caring teacher until was able to support himself and thrive. However, for undisclosed reasons, he had asked his mother to keep his background secret, and in exchange, he gave her an annual stipend of thirty pounds. Mrs. Pegler, for her part, had stayed away and visited only once a year, admiring his success from a distance.

Mr. Bounderby and Mrs. Sparsit look foolish—None of this was obvious at first, which led Mr. Gradgrind to innocently challenge her based on the stories told him by Bounderby, who had been lying about his past all along. That put Mr. Gradgrind in an awkward position, and following Mrs. Pegler's explanation and reprimand, it left Mr. Bounderby in an even more embarrassing condition. His life, it turned out, was one big pretense. He didn't feel like explaining himself, though, so he shooed the Coketown crowd off his chairs and out of his residence. But it was obvious to everyone that he was the biggest fool in the room, with Mrs. Sparsit a close second.

The new information sheds a different light on the situation with Stephen—As Sissy and Rachael made their way to Stone Lodge, they were accompanied by Mr. Gradgrind, who voiced his opinion that this new information about Mrs. Pegler should work in Stephen's favor. Young Tom, for his part, had hovered close to Bounderby throughout the evening, as though he meant to keep close watch over whatever information came before him. That way, he could prevent any undesired discoveries. His other tactic, intended as a diversion, was to exclaim loudly about Stephen's absence, apparently to make him seem guilty and draw the attention away from himself. It didn't entirely work. His sister, whom he now avoided, harbored vague, unacknowledged suspicions about him, and so did Sissy—though they never spoke about their feelings.

Chapter 6—The Starlight

Rachael and Sissy take a trip to the country—For those yearning to get away from the pollution of Coketown, there was the option of taking the train to one of the more outlying country areas to get a breath of fresh air. That was what Sissy and Rachael did that Sunday morning, when they ventured to a stop about halfway between Coketown and Bounderby's country home, and they were rewarded with a clear, crisp, sunny autumn day.

Mounds and hidden pits in the countryside—The countryside provided a nice break from Coketown's soot and chimneystacks and endless noise and motion. There were trees and birds and fresh smells, and everywhere—aside from occasional pile of coal—there was green grass. At times, they would come across the ruins of old works or a rotting fence. Sometimes, too, they would spot jumbled mounds of brambles, weeds, and tall grasses, but they had heard that these often masked dangerous pits, so they kept their distance from them.

Sissy and Rachael discover Stephen's hat and a deep, hidden pit—At noon, they rested, and as they looked around, it seemed that they were the only ones for miles and miles. But as Sissy was commenting on this, she noticed what looked like a freshly broken piece of fence, and as she came near to inspect it, she suddenly started and ran back to Rachael, who was already heading her way. Sissy had spotted a hat, which Rachael, now trembling, bent over to pick up. Written inside the hat in his own writing was Stephen's name, and on seeing it, Rachael broke into tears. There was no sign of blood or foul play, though, so Sissy determined to examine the area a little further. As she began to move forward, Rachael suddenly grabbed her and screamed. The grass had been hiding a deep pit. One step farther, and Sissy would have fallen in.

The two women run in opposite directions for help—Since Rachael was still screaming, Sissy's first move was to calm her down, reminding her that Stephen might still be alive and that they needed to help him. First, she tried calling down into the shaft numerous times, but with no reply. After throwing down a piece of earth and hearing no sound, she determined that they should run for help as fast as they could, each going in opposite directions.

Sissy finds help and sends a message by post to Louisa—After checking in different places, Sissy finally came to an engine-house shed, where she found two men sleeping. Still in a panic, she did her best to wake them and tell her story. One of the men had been drunk, but as soon as he understood what had happened, he sobered himself up by soaking his head in muddy water. On they ran, gathering together all the townspeople and whatever instruments were needed to rescue Stephen from the Old Hell Shaft. Sissy even sent a written message to Louisa, instructing the messenger to ride at top speed.

The townspeople gather, and a rescue party is organized—After what seemed like many hours away from the shaft, Sissy returned as quickly as she could, bringing with her some of the men she had found. While they waited for the necessary instruments, the men examined the area and tried calling down into the shaft, but with no luck. Gradually, stray onlookers collected around the pit, and finally the necessary tools arrived. Rachael, too, arrived with another group of people, including a surgeon who came equipped with medicine and wine. Enough people had gathered by now that the sobered-up man, who had been given a leadership position, placed limits on who could go beyond a certain point near the shaft. The idea was to prevent people from interfering with the rescue work, so other than those directly involved, only Sissy, Rachael, and later, the Gradgrind and Bounderby parties were allowed in.

Stephen is alive but badly hurt; the town surgeon has a makeshift bed made—By the time the equipment was ready to lower the two volunteers into the pit, it was already late afternoon. One of those who went down was the man who had sobered himself up, and he was also the first to come back up and relay the news: Stephen was alive but badly hurt, so much so that they needed to consult with the surgeon to determine the best way to bring him back up. By the time they lowered the man back down with the wine and some other items, the sun was already setting. In the meantime, the people constructed a makeshift bed with the guidance of the surgeon, and once the sobered-up man had returned to the surface, they lowered him back down again with the bed, a concoction of random clothes, straw, shawls, handkerchiefs, and other things.

Stephen fell into the pit on his way to Bounderby's country home by night—Apparently, Stephen had fallen onto a heap of trash and some earth and had landed one arm, which remained under his body. He had barely moved since his fall, except to maneuver some crumbs of bread and meat from his pocket to his mouth with his free arm. When he fell into the pit, he had been on his way to Bounderby's, having received Rachael's message and left immediately after work. Determined to clear his name, he had left in the dark and had not seen the pit. According to the pitman, his chances of survival were not good. The Old Hell Shaft, which had claimed many lives and now had ruined Stephen's, was aptly named.

A rescued but badly wounded Stephen speaks of his realizations down in the pit—Finally, they brought up Old Stephen in a crumpled heap, eliciting gasps and tears from the gathered crowd. The surgeon did his best to first make Stephen comfortable, and then he motioned to Rachael and Sissy to come near. Stephen's right hand, broken from the fall, lay on top of the covers, and his face looked up at the night sky. Rachael kneeled down beside him, placed her face directly over his, since he could not turn his head, and took his hand in hers. Even before he saw her, Old Stephen smiled and spoke her name. Now, as she took his hand, he did so again, and in his sweet, simple manner, he told her to not let go. He seemed to her to be in terrible pain, but he had already moved beyond it, though he had suffered long. Now he simply voiced his habitual understanding that the whole affair was one big "muddle." He had seen firsthand the hellish conditions in the pit, so he thoroughly understood the torturous circumstances so many men had worked in, circumstances that cost them their lives and robbed their families of husbands and fathers. He understood that the people had begged those who made the laws to treat them as human beings. Their lives were regarded as dispensable, and often they died without cause. Yet his tone bore no anger or resentment: he was simply relating things as they were.

Everything's a muddle—Old Stephen, so gentle and patient despite all, knew that he was dying. He spoke of being near to Rachael's younger sister, who had died many years ago, crippled and sickly. And he spoke lovingly of Rachael's patience and all that she had done for her sister as long as she was alive. It seemed to him that her sister's death had been, like so many things, unnecessary—the result of pollution and miserable living conditions. The same was true of his present state, which was the result of things being amiss. Had things been right and just, his fellow workers would not have misjudged him; Mr. Bounderby would not have suspected him, and he would not be lying there now, a crumpled heap.

Stephen speaks to Rachael of the guiding star—Suddenly, he turned Rachael's attention to the night sky, and looking up, she saw that his eyes were fixed on a star. That star, he said, had shone down upon him in his pain and taught him forgiveness. When he fell into the pit, he had been on his way to Bounderby's to clear his name. In that moment, he had been angry, suspecting Louisa and young Tom to have plotted against him together. But as he lay hurt in the pit, with the star shining down upon him and with thoughts of his beloved Rachael, his mind and heart gradually cleared, and he came to realize the need for forgiveness on all parts, and that thought became his prayer.

Stephen charges Mr. Gradgrind with clearing his name—Unbeknownst to Stephen, Louisa had been standing near him most of this time, and now she made her presence known. Seeing her, he realized that she'd heard his speech, but she gently assured him that they shared the same deep desire for understanding and forgiveness. Old Stephen then asked her to fetch her father. When Mr. Gradgrind arrived, Stephen asked him to take the responsibility for clearing his name. Perplexed, Mr. Gradgrind asked him how. The answer was that young Tom would inform him of that. The only information Stephen gave the father was that he had spoken with his son one evening. Now he placed his trust in the father to clear his name.

Stephen's last words—The time had come to bear the litter away, and as the carriers prepared to do so, Stephen again spoke to Rachael about the star. He had often thought, as he lay there in pain with the star above him in the sky, that it must be the same star that had guided the Wise Men and shepherds to the manger. When the litter-bearers seemed to carry him in the star's direction, his joy overflowed. And as Rachael held his hand, he asked her once more to not let go. That night, he said, they would walk together. Gentle and loving as ever, Rachael replied that she would walk with him the whole way. As he blessed her, Stephen's last request was that someone should cover his face.

Stephen goes to his Lord—With extraordinary care, the litter-bearers carried Old Stephen across the wide-open fields. They walked in silence and sadness, and Rachael never let go of his hand. Above them, in the night sky, the star that had been his companion in pain and had shown him the way of forgiveness now led him out of his suffering to his Lord.

Chapter 7—Whelp-hunting

Sissy whispers something to young Tom right before he disappears—Before the circle of onlookers had dispersed, young Tom—now regularly referred to as "the whelp"—had already disappeared. Just before that, Sissy, in response to the conversation between Old Stephen and Mr. Gradgrind, had left her previous place to whisper something in young Tom's ear.

Tom is missing—That night, Mr. Gradgrind, now charged with clearing Stephen's name, immediately sent for Tom after arriving back at Stone Lodge. When he discovered from Bounderby that Tom was missing from his usual place, he checked the bank in the morning, with the same disappointing result.

Mr. Gradgrind's deep change of heart—Not knowing what to do, Mr. Gradgrind returned home and locked himself in his study for the rest of the day and night, not even coming out to take food or opening the door to let anyone in. The next morning, he resumed his usual schedule, but it was clear that the previous day's events had taken their toll on him. Yet Mr. Gradgrind had learned some valuable life lessons that had deepened and improved him as a human being. Louisa assured him that his younger children would turn out better, and even she, his eldest daughter, would become a better person.

Mr. Gradgrind's desire to save his son—Mr. Gradgrind was still having difficulty processing the event—the robbery, the setup incriminating Stephen, and the overall wretchedness of young Tom's character. Now his fatherly desire was to try to save this wretched son of his, though he was also sworn to keep his promise to clear Stephen's name. Where would he begin? Time was short, and he had no idea where to find Tom.

Sissy's foresight enables them to find Tom—However, Sissy did. Louisa promptly told her father that Sissy, in her moment of whispered communication with Tom, had set things up so that Tom had a temporary hiding place and his family would know where to look for him. Mr. Gradgrind gratefully acknowledged Sissy. Somehow, he noted with tenderness, whenever there was a problem to solve, Sissy was there to facilitate it. Sissy explained that she and Louisa had had their suspicions, so when she heard Old Stephen's final request, she quickly told Tom to go at once to Sleary's circus, where she was sure he could hide. That news relieved Mr. Gradgrind, whose hope was to send his son abroad, where he could escape the dreadful fate that otherwise awaited him there in Coketown. The three of them agreed that, to prevent suspicion, Sissy and Louisa should go to Sleary's by a different route from

Mr. Gradgrind and that they should also arrive first, since their presence was less likely to be misconstrued.

Louisa and Sissy travel to Sleary's Horse-Riding show—After traveling all night and half the day, with little to eat and no rest, not to mention rough terrain in places, Sissy and Louisa finally found Sleary's circus twenty miles from where they had originally expected it. To avoid unwanted attention, they decided to purchase tickets, just like all the other spectators. Their goal was to give Mr. Sleary a discreet way of identifying them, whether he was selling tickets or performing in the ring. As it turned out, Master Kidderminster, now grown to manhood, was in charge of the money; but since that was his only focus, he failed to notice Sissy. Mr. Sleary arrived in the ring with his daughter Josephine as he led her in on her horse to perform her Tyrolean Flower Act. It didn't take long for them both to recognize Sissy, and as soon as the act was over, Sissy and Louisa were ushered into a little room, where Mr. Sleary received them.

Mr. Sleary welcomes Sissy—Mr. Sleary was always happy to see Sissy (or "Thethilia," as he called her, in his lisping accent). Being a shrewd man, he knew that she and Louisa had come with a definite intention. But he also understood the human spirit, so after reciting the full list of who had married and begotten whom, he insisted on showing Sissy to "her people." It was an intriguing but heartening spectacle for Louisa to watch—these circus people, with their healthy color and barely clothed bodies, warmly exchanging kisses, hugs, and greetings with Sissy.

Sleary informs them of Tom's disguise and his own commitment to help—When it was all over, and everyone had left, Mr. Sleary discreetly asked about the point of their visit. The young lady with Sissy, he guessed, must be the daughter of Mr. Gradgrind ("the Thquire"). Louisa confirmed this and quickly asked whether her brother was safe. Perfectly safe, came the answer, and taking them over to a hole in the wall where they could look into the ring, Mr. Sleary pointed out various circus characters in costume. He added that he understood that Mr. Gradgrind and he had their differing perspectives, and he was not keen to know what Tom had done. But one thing was certain: Mr. Gradgrind had taken in Sissy when she was in need, so he would now repay the favor. Turning their attention to the circus performers, he informed them that Tom was disguised as a black servant. Hearing this, Louisa gasped, but she immediately realized it was the perfect disguise. Mr. Sleary would leave Tom in costume until after Mr. Gradgrind's arrival, and once the performance was over, they could have the place to themselves.

Mr. Gradgrind connects with Mr. Sleary and composes a letter of passage for Tom—Mr. Gradgrind made it there shortly afterwards. Relieved to learn of Mr. Sleary's efforts, he now composed a letter ensuring his son passage from Liverpool, which was near the circus site, to some far-off continent. Tom would have to go alone since the presence of any one of them could easily identify him.

Mr. Gradgrind confronts his son—After waiting for the whole circus to clear out—audience, performers, and animals—they noticed Sleary taking his place by one of the circus doors, where he sat down to smoke. As they cautiously approached, he greeted Mr. Gradgrind and informed him that he would be there if he needed him and not to be put off by his son's costume. Once inside, Mr. Gradgrind took a seat on the clown's chair in the center of the ring. From there, all the way in the back in the dimly lit uppermost bleachers, he could see his son, miserable as ever. He was dressed in one of the most ridiculous, flea-bitten outfits he had ever seen, and the black grease on his face was beginning to streak. All that education and training come to this!

Tom explains himself—At first, young Tom refused to come down, but Sissy eventually managed to convince him to do so. How, his father wanted to know, had he managed to rob the bank? Tom bluntly told him that he had forced the safe, faked the use of a key, and secretly stashed the money he was supposed to be putting in the safe. Shocked by his son's actions, his father told him that a thunderbolt would have been easier to take. But Tom, in his growling way, was unimpressed. Hadn't his father taught them that a given number of people were bound to be dishonest? Wasn't that a law, and if so, how was he expected to avoid it? With a total lack of compassion, he added that if his father had reassured others with his philosophy, he should now do the same for himself. Baffled by his son's complete lack of moral perspective, Mr. Gradgrind hid his face, holding his head with his hands, as he had done so many times in the past few weeks. Finally, he informed Tom that they needed to get him to Liverpool, from there to be shipped overseas. His sullen answer was that if he had to do it, it couldn't possibly make him more miserable than he had been all his life.

Mr. Sleary unveils his escape plan; father and son say goodbye—Next, Gradgrind called Mr. Sleary to determine how to get Tom to Liverpool. Mr. Sleary, for his part, had already worked it all out in his mind. First, he would change Tom from a black slave into a joskin, or country bumpkin. The change of clothing was ready to go, and he would use beer—the best grease cleaner he knew—to wipe off his make-up. In half an hour, there would be a coach bound for the mail train, which would go straight to Liverpool. Sleary himself would accompany him, as a decoy. Gradgrind immediately agreed to these measures, and the necessary preparations were all accomplished in a few minutes. And so, as Thomas Gradgrind, Sr. handed his wayward son the letter he had written, he admonished him to mend his thinking and his actions, which had brought so much sorrow. His final words to Tom were that he forgave him and that he hoped that God would do the same.

Tom resents and avoids Louisa, but Louisa loves and forgives him—In a rare moment, Tom actually shed some tears over his father's words but refused to accept his sister's embrace, having rejected her out of hand. His perspective on her actions was totally selfish, making him unable to view her compassionately or to interpret anything she had done as loving. But Louisa, from the depths of her heart, forgave him and hoped that her words might some day ring true.

Bitzer ruins it all—Just moments before, Mr. Sleary had alerted them that it was time to go … but now there was a problem. Bitzer had arrived, panting and pale. He had come to take Tom into custody. He had his own reasons, and he was not about to let him escape—especially not by means of horseback riders. And with that, he grabbed Tom by the collar.

Chapter 8—Philosophy

Mr. Gradgrind questions Bitzer's lack of compassion—This new confrontation with Bitzer drove the party back into the ring, with Mr. Sleary guarding the door. Did he not have a heart? Mr. Gradgrind asked, dejected. Bitzer's answer was mechanical: everybody had a heart—that was what kept the circulation going. But was it capable of compassion? was the reply. No, it was only open to reason. Bitzer had learned his lessons too well, and Mr. Gradgrind now faced him in disbelief at his lack of human understanding and kindness. What could possibly motivate him to be so cruel toward a family?

Bitzer's belief in self-interest and his goal to obtain Tom's position—Bitzer's reasoned answer was entirely self-interested, and he made no apologies for it. He had been trained to believe that self-interest was a logical and desirable trait, so why shouldn't he pursue it? In fact, he had suspected Tom for a long time, and now he was merely bringing his suspicions and observations to fruition. If he could bring Tom in, he would get Tom's position, and he wasn't about to pass up that opportunity.

Bitzer's thorough training in the philosophy of facts backfires on Mr. Gradgrind—Seeing what he was dealing with, Mr. Gradgrind asked Bitzer if there was a price that could dissuade him from his current action. But Bitzer had already anticipated the question and calculated the value of the promotion, and he had determined that a promotion was a much safer and wiser route than aiding and abetting a crime. Desperate, Mr. Gradgrind tried appealing to Bitzer's sense of indebtedness for his education. But Bitzer felt no such sense. His education had been paid for, and hadn't Mr. Gradgrind taught them that all debts should be paid and nothing owed? Therefore, he owed him nothing. His purely economic reasoning was interrupted by Sissy and Louisa's sobs, which had a disturbing effect on him. In his opinion, it was pointless for them to do so. Besides, he had no hard feelings against Tom—he was just doing what was reasonable and useful.

Mr. Sleary's clever pretense—At this point, Mr. Sleary came forward. He had been listening attentively to the whole conversation and now added his two bits. Until now, he had not been aware of what Tom had done, but now that he knew, he could not agree to be a part of it. However, he would at least be willing to drive Tom and Bitzer to the station, and in the meantime, he could hide the matter from the townspeople. More than that, though, was not possible since Bitzer was, after all, right.

Sleary's back-up escape plan—Feeling abandoned by what had seemed their last hope, Mr. Gradgrind and Louisa were even more dejected than before. But Mr. Sleary was a clever and faithful man. With his one good eye, he motioned to Sissy to stay while the others left. She had not been fooled by his last speech, so what he said next came as no surprise. The "Thquire" had been faithful to her, and he would do the same for him now. Besides, Bitzer was the type of person that Sleary's people were inclined to throw out the window because of his attitude. But Sleary had a plan. If Sissy would alert Tom, the following would be put into action: when Sleary's trained horse began to dance, Tom was to jump on a fast-moving pony coach driven by Childers, while a trained dog kept Bitzer at bay. If the horse and the dog didn't do their part, Sleary would disown them—"Sharp's the word!" he added, in his lisp (he always said that when he meant business).

The plan succeeds; Mr. Gradgrind expresses his deep gratitude—At eight in the morning the following day, Mr. Sleary met Mr. Gradgrind, Louisa, and Sissy, who had been waiting up all night to hear the outcome. The plan had been successful, and by now Tom should be on his way to another country. Deeply grateful, Mr. Gradgrind hinted that a monetary reward was in order. But Mr. Sleary, always thinking first of his people and his animals, outlined what he thought might be useful and enjoyable for them: £5 for Childers' family, a dog collar, horse's bells, a banquet with alcoholic beverages for the company. For himself, all he wished for was a little brandy and water. Mr. Gradgrind was concerned that it was not enough of a repayment, so Sleary added that he could even the score by occasionally engaging the horse riders for a performance.

Sleary privately tells Mr. Gradgrind an extraordinary tale—Having made his requests, Sleary asked the young ladies to excuse him and Mr. Gradgrind for a moment, since he had something to tell him in private. However, before getting to the main point of his statement, Mr. Sleary led up to it with a colorful but puzzling description of the amazing instinct that dogs have for finding people. Mr. Gradgrind listened patiently and attentively but wasn't sure of Mr. Sleary's point until he described an incident that took place just over a year ago. An old, nearly blind and lame dog, which had clearly traveled many miles, came into the ring searching for a specific child. Mr. Sleary deduced this from the fact that it inspected each of the horse riders' children one by one. Finally, when it came to Mr. Sleary, it did something extraordinary. As exhausted as it was from its travels, it did a handstand with it forelegs, and after wagging its tail, it fell down dead. In that moment, Sleary recognized the dog as Merrylegs.

The dog's arrival signals the death of Sissy's father; Sleary decides not to tell Sissy—Mr. Gradgrind immediately recalled the name of the dog that had belonged to Sissy's father. Mr. Sleary continued, saying that he knew that the dog's return in that manner meant that Sissy's father was dead. After a long discussion between himself, his daughter Josephine, and her husband Childers, they concluded that it would be best to not tell Sissy. It would add nothing helpful to her life and only create pain. No one would ever know why her father deserted her, whether out of irresponsibility or to spare her from the burden of his own pain. Mr. Gradgrind mentioned that she still kept the bottle of oil she had purchased for her father so many years ago. In his view, she would never, for the rest of her life, let go of her belief in his love.

Sleary's profound observations on love—Sleary's response to this is one of the most profound statements in the entire book. The fact that Dickens uses Sleary's character, with his comical lisp and his ever-present brandy and water, to deliver this speech is itself a statement that the depths of existence cannot be fathomed by the shallowness of appearances. Pondering his drink, he observed that the situation with Sissy and her father's dog seemed to suggest two things: that there was indeed such a thing as love, something that went far beyond self-interest; and that this love had its own rules, its own means of determining value and sometimes of forgoing calculation altogether. But just as dogs had their special, incomprehensible ways of finding people, this thing called love was equally hard to pinpoint or understand.

Sleary bids them all farewell and leaves Mr. Gradgrind with humane words of advice—Mr. Gradgrind said nothing as Mr. Sleary finished his brandy and called Louisa and Sissy back into the room. Bidding each one farewell, he kissed Sissy and commended and thanked Louisa for her sisterly trust and goodwill, and he hoped that Tom would grow to be a better a brother and person. As he shook Mr. Gradgrind's hand, he reminded him once more to avoid judging the circus life. Entertainers were also a part of existence, as necessary as working and studying, and it was best to see them in a kind and understanding light. In his parting comic line, he exclaimed how he never knew he could talk so much!

Chapter 9—Final

Bounderby decides to terminate Mrs. Sparsit—Mr. Bounderby's inflated sense of self would not tolerate any contradictions, so when Mrs. Sparsit uncovered the truth of his family background, she ceased to serve her purpose as an ego support and became instead a thorn in his side. Somehow he had to salvage his injured self-image, and after much thought, he determined that the best way to do that would be to dismiss her from his service. In his view, she was still in a position of dependency, while he was in a position of power, and this would be his way of getting back at her.

A mutually disdainful parting—Since the awkward occasion of the discovery of his mother, Mr. Bounderby's interaction with Mrs. Sparsit had been uncomfortable. She adopted a mournful, apologetic attitude on the surface, and this only annoyed him further and fostered an abrupt approach in dealing with her. One day, at lunch, his annoyance reached a head, and after insulting her (specifically, her nose), he threw his knife down on the table. Mrs. Sparsit perceived that she was the object of this tantrum and decided it would be best if she went to her own apartment at the bank. Mr. Bounderby took the opportunity to accompany her to the door and inform her in a polite but disdainful manner that she would no longer be a part of his household. Essentially, he told her that there was no room in his home for someone of her prying nature to be meddling in his affairs and that she should do so elsewhere—at Lady Scadgers', for example. Of course, Mrs. Sparsit was convinced of her superiority to the last, and after scornfully laughing at Mr. Bounderby and making sarcastic references to his judgment, she informed him that she had never referred to his portrait as anything other than a "Noodle" and that a "Noodle" was worthy of nothing but disdain. Thus ended the Bounderby-Sparsit relationship.

A summary of the different characters' fates—The remainder of this final chapter of *Hard Times* looks into the future of each character and relates their ultimate outcomes. It does not try to mitigate or sugarcoat things but portrays each fate in relation to the thoughts adopted by the individual characters, combined with their prior mental and moral history. And while the thread of Christian thinking has not been hidden, it becomes most obvious in certain sections of this final chapter.

Bounderby's vision of a meager, unpleasant future for Mrs. Sparsit—The look into the future began with Mr. Bounderby, who was left gazing into the fire after Mrs. Sparsit's dramatic departure. Mrs. Sparsit's own future was not aided by her arrogance. She was left to live in cramped quarters with Lady Scadgers, where they would battle out their differences and exhaust their limited income on a regular basis. This much he was able to see.

Bounderby's limited time—The question was: how much could he see of his own future? Could he see himself aggrandizing Bitzer for his efforts to capture Tom? Could he foresee future versions of himself taking his place as the inflated, self-congratulatory new masters of Coketown, all brought about by the creation of his will, which would take effect on his death from a seizure five years from then?

Mr. Gradgrind's change of heart and the deepening of his philosophy—Mr. Gradgrind, too, would find his future deeply affected by recent events. He would learn from his experiences, as he had already begun to do, that facts were not enough and that Faith, Hope, and Love were necessary ingredients that could not be negated or enslaved by hard, cold calculation. For this recognition, he would lose his good reputation among his political colleagues, who valued only each other and cared nothing for the working people—to them, a mere idea—or for those who supported them. Unlike Mr. Bounderby, Mr. Gradgrind was relatively clear-sighted, and it was likely that he foresaw this outcome.

Visions of the future, real and unreal—Dickens structures this section so that he visits each character on the same day (or evening), the day of Mr. Bounderby's and Mrs. Sparsit's break-up. Mr. Bounderby, as we know, was left staring into the fire; Mr. Gradgrind pondered his life in his study; and now, in the evening, Louisa too sat looking into the fire, with a soul less caged by the tyranny of facts and calculation. What did she see? Dickens asks. She knew that her father would keep his word and publish both Stephen's innocence and his own son's guilt, painful though that might be. That much was clear. But there were other things that she may or may not have seen, some of them true, some of them not. There was Rachael's illness and eventual recovery; her return to work; her compassion for Stephen's drunken ex-wife; her hardworking lot in life; her deep humility. There was her brother, now far away, who came to understand the truth of her prediction that her love would someday mean a fantastic deal to him. He conveyed these thoughts through letters, but before he could express them in person, he died en route. There was her vision of herself remarried, a wife and mother, taking care that her children should experience the childhood she never had. But this was just a vision and never came about. For Sissy, though, that same vision of love and innocence, of imagination and beauty, was to be the natural outcome of her natural way of being. She would continue being a light to the impoverished inhabitants of Coketown, to add joy to their lives and prevent them from falling into the dreary state that was once the norm.

Dickens's final note to the reader—The final paragraph of the novel is directly addressed to the reader and comes off as a bit cryptic at first. It seems to be saying that if Dickens and the reader have learned the book's lessons well, they will know to approach life with greater compassion and a lighter, easier spirit.

28047841R00075

Printed in Great Britain
by Amazon